Evaluating Training Programs in Business and Industry

Robert O. Brinkerhoff, *Editor*
Western Michigan University, Kalamazoo

NEW DIRECTIONS FOR PROGRAM EVALUATION
A Publication of the American Evaluation Association
A joint organization of the Evaluation Research Society and the Evaluation Network

NICK L. SMITH, *Editor-in-Chief*
Syracuse University

Number 44, Winter 1989

Paperback sourcebooks in
The Jossey-Bass Higher Education
and Social and Behavioral Science Series

Jossey-Bass Inc., Publishers
San Francisco • Oxford

Robert O. Brinkerhoff (ed.).
Evaluating Training Programs in Business and Industry.
New Directions for Program Evaluation, no. 44.
San Francisco: Jossey-Bass, 1989.

New Directions for Program Evaluation Series
A publication of the American Evaluation Association
Nick L. Smith, *Editor-in-Chief*

Copyright © 1989 by Jossey-Bass Inc., Publishers

Copyright under International, Pan American, and Universal Copyright Conventions. All rights reserved. No part of this issue may be reproduced in any form—except for brief quotation (not to exceed 500 words) in a review or professional work—without permission in writing from the publishers.

New Directions for Program Evaluation is published quarterly by Jossey-Bass Inc., Publishers (publication number USPS 449-050) and is sponsored by the American Evaluation Association. POSTMASTER: Send address changes to Jossey-Bass Inc., Publishers, 350 Sansome Street, San Francisco, California 94104.

Editorial correspondence should be sent to the Editor-in-Chief, Nick L. Smith, School of Education, Syracuse University, 330 Huntington Hall, Syracuse, N.Y. 13244-2340.

Library of Congress Catalog Card Number LC 85-644749

International Standard Serial Number ISSN 0164-7989

International Standard Book Number ISBN 1-55542-859-X

Cover art by WILLI BAUM

Manufactured in the United States of America. Printed on acid-free paper.

Ordering Information

The paperback sourcebooks listed below are published quarterly and can be ordered either by subscription or single copy.

Subscriptions cost $64.00 per year for institutions, agencies, and libraries. Individuals can subscribe at the special rate of $48.00 per year *if payment is by personal check.* (Note that the full rate of $64.00 applies if payment is by institutional check, even if the subscription is designated for an individual.) Standing orders are accepted.

Single copies are available at $14.95 when payment accompanies order. (California, New Jersey, New York, and Washington, D.C., residents please include appropriate sales tax.) For billed orders, cost per copy is $14.95 plus postage and handling.

Substantial discounts are offered to organizations and individuals wishing to purchase bulk quantities of Jossey-Bass sourcebooks. Please inquire.

Please note that these prices are for the calendar year 1989 and are subject to change without prior notice. Also, some titles may be out of print and therefore not available for sale.

To ensure correct and prompt delivery, all orders must give either the *name of an individual* or an *official purchase order number.* Please submit your order as follows:

Subscriptions: specify series and year subscription is to begin.
Single copies: specify sourcebook code (such as PE1) and first two words of title.

Mail all orders to:
Jossey-Bass Inc., Publishers
350 Sansome Street
San Francisco, California 94104

New Directions for Program Evaluation Series
Nick L. Smith, *Editor-in-Chief*

PE1 *Exploring Purposes and Dimensions,* Scarvia B. Anderson, Claire D. Coles
PE2 *Evaluating Federally Sponsored Programs,* Charlotte C. Rentz, R. Robert Rentz
PE3 *Monitoring Ongoing Programs,* Donald L. Grant
PE4 *Secondary Analysis,* Robert F. Boruch

PE5   *Utilization of Evaluative Information,* Larry A. Braskamp, Robert D. Brown
PE6   *Measuring the Hard-to-Measure,* Edward H. Loveland
PE7   *Values, Ethics, and Standards in Evaluation,* Robert Perloff, Evelyn Perloff
PE8   *Training Program Evaluators,* Lee Sechrest
PE9   *Assessing and Interpreting Outcomes,* Samuel Ball
PE10 *Evaluation of Complex Systems,* Ronald J. Wooldridge
PE11 *Measuring Effectiveness,* Dan Baugher
PE12 *Federal Efforts to Develop New Evaluation Methods,* Nick L. Smith
PE13 *Field Assessments of Innovative Evaluation Methods,* Nick L. Smith
PE14 *Making Evaluation Research Useful to Congress,* Leonard Saxe, Daniel Koretz
PE15 *Standards for Evaluation Practice,* Peter H. Rossi
PE16 *Applications of Time Series Analysis to Evaluation,* Garlie A. Forehand
PE17 *Stakeholder-Based Evaluation,* Anthony S. Bryk
PE18 *Management and Organization of Program Evaluation,* Robert G. St. Pierre
PE19 *Philosophy of Evaluation,* Ernest R. House
PE20 *Developing Effective Internal Evaluation,* Arnold J. Love
PE21 *Making Effective Use of Mailed Questionnaires,* Daniel C. Lockhart
PE22 *Secondary Analysis of Available Data Bases,* David J. Bowering
PE23 *Evaluating the New Information Technologies,* Jerome Johnston
PE24 *Issues in Data Synthesis,* William H. Yeaton, Paul M. Wortman
PE25 *Culture and Evaluation,* Michael Quinn Patton
PE26 *Economic Evaluations of Public Programs,* James S. Catterall
PE27 *Utilizing Prior Research in Evaluation Planning,* David S. Cordray
PE28 *Randomization and Field Experimentation,* Robert F. Boruch, Werner Wothke
PE29 *Teaching of Evaluation Across the Disciplines,* Barbara Gross Davis
PE30 *Naturalistic Evaluation,* David D. Williams
PE31 *Advances in Quasi-Experimental Design and Analysis,* William M. K. Trochim
PE32 *Measuring Efficiency: An Assessment of Data Envelopment Analysis,* Richard H. Silkman
PE33 *Using Program Theory in Evaluation,* Leonard Bickman
PE34 *Evaluation Practice in Review,* David S. Cordray, Howard S. Bloom, Richard J. Light
PE35 *Multiple Methods in Program Evaluation,* Melvin M. Mark, R. Lance Shotland
PE36 *The Client Perspective on Evaluation,* Jeri Nowakowski
PE37 *Lessons from Selected Program and Policy Areas,* Howard S. Bloom, David S. Cordray, Richard J. Light
PE38 *Timely, Lost-Cost Evaluation in the Public Sector,* Christopher G. Wye, Harry P. Hatry
PE39 *Evaluation Utilization,* John A. McLaughlin, Larry J. Weber, Robert W. Covert, Robert B. Ingle
PE40 *Evaluating Program Environments,* Kendon J. Conrad, Cynthia Roberts-Gray
PE41 *Evaluation and the Federal Decision Maker,* Gerald L. Barkdoll, James B. Bell
PE42 *International Innovations in Evaluation Methodology,* Ross F. Conner, Michael Hendricks
PE43 *Evaluating Health Promotion Programs,* Marc T. Braverman

New Directions for Program Evaluation

Sponsored by the American Evaluation Association
(A Joint Organization of the Evaluation Research Society
and the Evaluation Network)

Editor-in-Chief:

Nick L. Smith, Education, Syracuse University

Editorial Assistant:

Prachee Mukherjee, Education, Syracuse University

Editorial Advisory Board:

Gerald L. Barkdoll, U.S. Food and Drug Administration, Washington, D.C.
Leonard B. Bickman, Program Evaluation Laboratory, Vanderbilt University
Robert F. Boruch, Psychology and Statistics, Northwestern University
Donald T. Campbell, Social Relations, Lehigh University
Thomas D. Cook, Psychology, Northwestern University
David S. Cordray, U.S. General Accounting Office, Washington, D.C.
David M. Fetterman, School of Education, Stanford University
Barry J. Fraser, Curtin University, Western Australia
Jennifer C. Greene, Human Service Studies, Cornell University
Edward H. Haertel, School of Education, Stanford University
Ernest R. House, School of Education, University of Colorado, Boulder
Michael H. Kean, CTB-McGraw-Hill, Monterey, California
Morris Lai, College of Education, University of Hawaii
Laura C. Leviton, Health Services Administration, University of Pittsburgh
Richard J. Light, Education, Harvard University
Mark W. Lipsey, Psychology, Claremont Graduate School
Jennifer McCreadie, Madison Metropolitan School District (Wisconsin)
Jack McKillip, Psychology, Southern Illinois University, Carbondale
Anna Madison, Public Affairs, Texas Southern University
Jeanne C. Marsh, School of Social Service Administration, University of Chicago
Carol T. Mowbray, Resident and Evaluation Division, Michigan Department of Mental Health
David Nevo, Education, Tel Aviv University

Dianna L. Newman, Evaluation Consortium, SUNY–Albany
Dennis Palumbo, School of Justice Studies, Arizona State University
Michael Q. Patton, Minnesota Extension Service,
University of Minnesota
Mark St. John, Inverness Research Associates, Inverness, California
Thomas A. Schwandt, Educational Psychology,
Northern Illinois University
Lee B. Sechrest, Psychology, University of Arizona
William R. Shadish, Jr., Psychology, Memphis State University
John K. Smith, Education, University of Northern Iowa
Charles B. Stalford, OERI, Washington, D.C.
Carol H. Weiss, Education, Harvard University

American Evaluation Association, 9555 Persimmon Tree Road, Potomac, MD 20854

Contents

Editor's Notes   1
Robert O. Brinkerhoff

1. Using Evaluation to Transform Training   5
Robert O. Brinkerhoff
This chapter presents an agenda for evaluation of training in the new competitive global market.

2. Evaluating the Merit and Worth of Sales Training: Asking the Right Questions   21
Dale M. Brethower
Training programs and results are strengthened when evaluators ask the right questions.

3. Using Evaluation to Build Commitment to Training   35
Stephen Joel Gill
Without substantial management commitment, training is not used to full organizational potential; this chapter shows how to build that commitment with evaluation.

4. Strategy for Internal Evaluators   45
Alan C. Nowakowski
Analyzing evaluation services in a business training environment serves as a vehicle for deriving internal evaluation strategy.

5. Evaluation of Training by Trainers   59
Nicholas M. Sanders
This chapter discusses the attitudinal and cultural obstacles that an evaluator confronts and presents some potential directions for doing a more complete job.

6. Everything Important in Business and Industry Is Evaluated   71
Richard A. Swanson
When evaluators understand the economic bases of training and the language and expectations of business, evaluation can proceed more effectively.

7. Evaluation and Business Issues: Tools for Management Decision Making   83
Dale C. Brandenburg
Linking business issues and decision making to training evaluation activities determines the overall success of training efforts.

Index   101

Editor's Notes

The profession of training has grown to tremendous proportions and is more pervasive in practice than ever before. Recent estimates (Carnevale, 1986; Eurich, 1985) indicate that American business and industry spend more than $30 billion annually to train and educate more than fifteen million people—about one out of every eight Americans. The investment by private industry in education and training now rivals, in scope and resources, the total public educational enterprise.

Yet, there are signs that the boom is ending. Several prominent corporations (IBM and AT&T, for example) have recently cut back their training departments. As global competition intensifies and the pressure on resources increases, trainers in all settings will be harder pressed than ever before to be more productive and more accountable for their results. The days of the richly endowed training department with its fat program catalogs are numbered. Training practices of the future are likely to be leaner in scope than present procedures. That is, the training will be less extensive and more tightly focused on smaller, strategically selected groups of employees, needs-driven programming, and thoroughly cost-justified proposals.

The stakes are high and bear not only on the survival of training but also on the very survival of organizations. The rapid pace of technological change, the shrinking labor pool, the shift to a service economy and orientation, and the expansion in competition put an increasingly high premium on human resource capacity. Training cannot merely make a difference, it can make *the* difference to business success or failure.

Evaluation may well be the key to the success of training in the future. Evaluation, if effectively applied, can help trainers squeeze the maximum amount from shrinking resources, and it can demonstrate the critical linkages between training's contribution to human performance and capacity and to organizational effectiveness. The challenges to and opportunities for evaluation are tremendous. But the risks are great also; for if evaluation is weak or poorly done, then the entire practice and profession of training are jeopardized.

Despite the need for their services, evaluators of training face tough going in the common organizational setting. There is not much support for formal evaluation of training (Gutek, 1988) in business and industry, and the typical training program receives only perfunctory and superficial assessment.

There are exceptions, however. Some companies invest heavily in evaluation of training. Some evaluation consultants keep very busy with training clients, and new books and articles on evaluation of training are emerging annually. In this issue of *New Directions for Program Evaluation,* current principles and practices are discussed by some of the busiest of the evaluation thinkers and practitioners.

This issue is intended to interest and serve all evaluators, not only evaluators of training. The practice of evaluation in the context of business and industry training programs warrants special attention, for evaluators of training have confronted problems common to all evaluators and have discovered some unique and innovative solutions. Before describing each of the chapters, I provide an overview of what I see as the major "lessons" taught in these pages.

In the profit-making, pragmatic corporate environment, evaluation has had to truly serve to survive. Corporate managers have little time for reading in the first place, and even less time for information they do not regard as direct, concise, and, above all, functional. Research, including those who conduct it, is seen as "academic" (a euphemism in business for "out of touch" or "worthless") and is viewed at best with mildly hostile suspicion. Further, in the business setting, unlike public education and social service, there have been no mandates or grants for evaluation. Here, evaluation has won its stripes the hard way: either add value or take a hike—put up or shut up.

To a great extent, evaluators in business settings have done more evaluation by doing less evaluation. That is, rather than try to win support for evaluation as a separate activity, they have sought ways to weave evaluation thinking and activities into already existing and valued operations (quality control and assurance, for example, or training-course development).

Evaluators in business and industry settings have worked hard to learn the language, needs, motives, and culture of their clients. In practice, this has entailed spending much time trying to understand the function of training and how it adds value to organizational performance. In my experience, those evaluators who have been especially successful have never viewed evaluation as a problem, as in "How can I get some evaluation done around here?" Rather, successful evaluators have seen the problem as, "How can I help my clients (trainers) be more effective?" The evaluation problem is not evaluation, it is training. Figure out how to do evaluation that will make training more effective and worthwhile, and you have solved the evaluation "problem."

These chapters demonstrate promising new directions and powerful practices in the evaluation of training. A common theme here is *utility.* All of the authors make their living, either completely or centrally, by applying evaluation to training operations. Although all the authors have solid academic grounding, their work reflects practicality and a deep appreciation for the needs and problems of practitioners. These authors represent different perspectives and approaches, but they are alike in one key respect: the evaluation they have done has worked—it has helped trainers become more effective and accountable.

The opening chapter reviews the recent growth in training and examines a number of issues and problems accompanying this growth. These concerns have special significance for the future of training, and thus, I believe, for evaluation. This chapter closes with an "agenda" for future evaluation of training efforts, much of which is addressed and expanded on in the following chapters.

The next four chapters take a close look at some particularly useful applications and perspectives. Two of these are provided by authors who consult with a variety of organizations, and two are provided by "insiders—full-time corporate employees. The final two chapters, whose authors are external consultants, return to consideration of conceptual issues that transcend particular applications.

In Chapter Two, Dale M. Brethower provides an incisive and entertaining discussion of how evaluators must be careful in identifying evaluation purposes and questions. Using sales training as an example, he explains the multiple stakeholder expectations for training and discusses how these formulate a diverse set of evaluation questions. Brethower includes specific and practical advice about how evaluators can, and should, avoid pursuing the wrong questions, which, he cautions, can be both enticing and destructive. A conceptual model and guidelines are provided that readers can use to help trainers (and other clients) focus their efforts for maximum utility.

In a similarly straightforward and practical manner, Stephen Joel Gill, in Chapter Three, presents strategies and techniques he has used to elicit and nurture management support for training. Without such support, training effects are rarely translated into individual and organizational benefits, thus Gill's evaluation applications are of special importance and interest. This chapter includes a management support model and a detailed example of its use in a large multi-national corporation.

Alan C. Nowakowski, in Chapter Four, offers an insider's view about how evaluation services can be focused to meet a relatively narrow but critically important dimension of training quality. This chapter provides a close look at how evaluators at the Arthur Andersen and Company, a major purveyor and user of training programs, design and conduct a course development evaluation. Nowakowski includes practical and detailed information about a useful evaluation method that has met specific and important business information needs.

Chapter Five is contributed by another "insider," Nicholas M. Sanders of Cigna Corporation. Sanders identifies and discusses the trainer attitudes and cultural barriers he has encountered as a practitioner in a corporate setting. He echoes and expands on some of the key points raised in the opening chapter by exploring problems with trainee satisfaction surveys and measures of learning. In particular, he shows how evaluators can serve such business interests as quality improvement and job performance by allying themselves with parallel corporate activities.

Chapter Six, by Richard A. Swanson, begins the "step back" from specific training applications to explore the business environment in which training is conducted. He provides a practical conceptual framework to help evaluators of training understand the critical economic foundation of training that characterizes the perspective of top management. Of special interest in this chapter are guidelines for trainers to understand the language of business and the performance measures that are of primary interest to corporate audiences.

In the final chapter, Dale C. Brandenburg brings us full circle by returning to the broad perspective of the opening chapter. Chapter Seven examines the conceptual roots of training evaluation. This examination includes an analysis of the range of evaluation applications that confront an evaluator of training and provides a useful framework for focusing evaluation at the proper level and on the purposes that will best serve the organization.

Robert O. Brinkerhoff
Editor

References

Carnevale, A. P. "The Learning Enterprise." *Training and Development Journal*, 1986, *45*, 18-26.
Eurich, N. P. *Corporate Classrooms*. Princeton, N.J.: Princeton University Press, 1985.
Gutek, S. P. "Training-Program Evaluation: An Investigation of Perceptions and Practices in Nonmanufacturing Business Organizations." Unpublished doctoral dissertation, Western Michigan University, 1988.

Robert O. Brinkerhoff is professor of Education at Western Michigan University, Kalamazoo, where he coordinates graduate programs in human resource development. He is a consultant with a wide range of corporations and organizations in the United States, Europe, Australia, and other countries.

Some important new directions for evaluation are presented that can help the training function add greater value and enhance organizational effectiveness.

Using Evaluation to Transform Training

Robert O. Brinkerhoff

The training and development function, and the profession itself, face unprecedented challenges in the coming decade. These challenges are masked, however, by the current boom in training. Organizations around the world are doing more training and spending more money than ever before on training and development. In the United States, for example, it is estimated (Carnevale, 1986; Eurich, 1985) that private industry now spends as much on education and training as the entire public school system. It is my belief, however, that unless leaders in training engage in far greater usage of evaluation and other quality improvement efforts than they now pursue, the training profession faces serious threats to its survival.

The Challenge

The challenge is to firmly establish training as a valued and productive business partner that makes effective contributions to competitive advantage. Unless such a business partnership is nurtured and demonstrated, training cannot survive. The challenge involves more than simply a charge to do more evaluation. The challenge is to do more of a different order of evaluation—proactive, directive evaluation that will lead the training profession and practice to a new level of operation and impact.

Before discussing the new sort of evaluation that is needed, it is important to look at the current state of the practice in today's corporate settings. My premise is that the changes in training over the past twenty years have led to a situation that is unprecedented in both risk and opportunity. The risk is that organizations are not now receiving and will not receive concomitantly high returns on their increased training investments. The opportunity is for evaluation to become a vital catalyst in the transformation of training.

I direct my attention in this chapter to business and industry settings, but the points I make are equally applicable to training functions in schools and universities, and in governmental and other public agencies. Likewise, when I state that training must become an effective "business" partner, I use the term generically to denote the purposes and operations of an organization. Thus, the business of a school is education of students, or the business of an adoption agency is the placement of children in loving homes, in the same sense that it is the business of the automobile industry to manufacture and sell automobiles while earning a profit.

Current Context

Fast Times at Corporate High. A number of trends and forces account for the current boom in training. As the plethora of recent literature about the new organizational context makes clear (Peters, 1985; Tichy, 1986; Hayes, 1985, for example), businesses and industries around the world are entering a new era. The transition to a global market and the introduction of new manufacturing technologies such as "just-in-time inventory" and computer-assisted design have brought immense competition and increasingly rapid product development cycles. As a result, demands for adaptable work forces that are proficient in new technologies are great. Managers, for example, must be masters at leading change, as opposed to simply skilled at administering new policies and procedures. Further, an increasing emphasis on quality and customer service demands new skills and sensitivities from employees across all levels of the organization (see Albrecht and Zemke, 1985; Desatnick, 1987). Customer satisfaction and service quality, which derive directly from the skills and attitudes of the work force, are often the key ingredients that propel an industry to dominance.

Labor shortages that promise to continue for many more years require organizations to change procedures and strategies while maintaining their employees. Organizations will need to change to survive but will be largely unable to hire new employees, thus requiring continuous training and retraining of a stable labor pool. At the same time, the organizational culture is making a transition to a "lifetime employment" approach. As companies compete for a shrinking number of qualified new hires, the availability of education and training programs becomes a lure, like salaries and benefits, for attracting recruits. Training, then, has come to be seen increasingly as a staff benefit at the same time as it has become a functional tool for creating competitive advantage.

While the training boom has been brewing and growing, training, and development have emerged as a profession, and as a common component of virtually every organization's bureaucracy. Today, training typically is centralized in a training department and often has high-level corporate visibility. Training departments regularly and vigorously recruit professional staff, and qualifications typically require academic preparation in education and training. Not surprisingly, preservice and in-service preparation programs for trainers have sprung up at dozens of colleges and universities.

Lastly, the tools of the training trade have become dramatically more sophisticated in recent years. Corporate training centers such as those maintained by Steelcase, Upjohn, IBM, Arthur Andersen, and Xerox, to name only a few, are extremely well equipped and designed to incorporate the latest in trainee conveniences as well as in learning technologies. Educators from public schools and universities are often dazzled, if not intimidated, by the clearly visible differences in resource allocation and relative opulence in the workplaces of their corporate cousins. Training programs in business and industry typically employ the latest in audio-visual equipment, computer-assisted learning technologies, and so forth. Vendor-supplied training programs incorporate generous amounts of network-quality videotapes and the glossiest of materials and supplies. Concomitantly, the expectations of trainees for training that is high quality, well designed, smooth running, and entertaining appear to be rising.

In sum, today's trainers appear to be living high on the hog. They are better supported than ever before and busier than ever before. And the future looks even brighter.

Bad News. There is a dark side to these good times. As it would take a special trip to see the backside of the Earth's moon, so it takes a special effort to see the dark side of the training boom. I see several trends and forces, as well as inherent aspects of training, that pose a recessionary threat to the practice and profession of training. Together, these form special challenges and a critical agenda for evaluators of training.

The Bureaucratization of Training. In today's organization, training is typically a separate division or unit within the bureaucratic hierarchy. It is virtually always separated administratively from line operations, and it may even be separately housed in its own building. There are, of course, certain advantages to separation. Corporate-centered training programs can address long-range developmental goals, for example, the kind that line managers, concerned with quarterly financial performance, would just as soon forgo. A separate training center also projects a "campus" feel and protects trainees from job interruptions.

But administrative separation is vulnerable to the threat that training operations will not be responsive to line operation needs, whether owing to benign ignorance, sinister empire-building interests, or both. As is the case in any bureaucracy, administrative units spend a certain, often increasing amount of time in maintaining and expanding their status. It is easy for such service units as training departments to lose sight of their ultimate purposes. When evaluations are not designed to aggressively assess and report progress toward organizational goals, these goals can increasingly fade into the noise of the bureaucratic background.

The Professionalization of Training. As noted previously, there is little doubt that the training of today is of higher instructional quality than past efforts. Training done several decades ago was most likely to be carried out by a relatively unsophisticated trainer using relatively unsophisticated instructional techniques. Yet, there was relatively far less training being done, and what training was being done was closely linked to business operations and to line management. Today, training staff and managers are likely to be training or personnel professionals, often with little experience in the business of the organization that supports them.

To be sure, professional trainers are knowledgeable of educational theory and practice, and they can typically design and conduct effective learning programs. But professionalization has resulted in a young, moderately experienced training staff, particularly in large organizations that offer career paths in training and other personnel specialties. As a result, trainers increasingly have little credibility with older, experience-wizened managers and employees, and not for false reasons. These professional trainers are likely to be most concerned with designing and delivering efficient training; such concerns for doing training "right" can easily grow to supplant concerns for doing the right training.

Program-Driven Versus Needs-Driven Curricula. The ascent of training to bureaucratic status has inevitably increased the probability that more and more training gets done not because it is needed but rather, for the same reason that mountains get climbed, because it is there. In many Fortune 500 companies with whom I have worked, I have asked administrators of training programs about the origins of the programs. Most have admitted that they were simply assigned to operate them and that they do not know when or why a decision was made to include their programs in their respective company's curriculum. The increasingly fat training-program catalogues in American companies grow the way that coral reefs do, by accumulation.

Robinson and Robinson (1989), in their recent book on training, distinguish between training administered as an *activity*, and training administered for business *impact*. Activity-driven training leaders are accountable for design and delivery of training programs, as opposed to the business results of training. Swanson (1982, 1987) presents a notion similar to the activity-impact distinction by observing that there are two basic foundations to training: psychology and economics. The psychological foundation has become predominant and focuses on the development and delivery of training, whereas the economic foundation focuses on needs assessment and contribution to organizational performance.

The perspectives defined by Swanson and Robinson and Robinson are readily apparent in practice. Anyone involved professionally in training in today's organizations cannot help but observe that the typical training practitioner is so busy organizing and delivering training that there is very little effort paid to needs assessment and other front-end analysis, or to follow-up assessment of training results. Keeping the training department stocked with the latest in vendor-supplied programs is a high priority, one that consumes increasing amounts of time simply to stay current both with vendors and with what one's competitor companies are purchasing. The "business" of the training department is increasingly seen, both by those within the department and eventually by those outside of it, as the design and delivery of training. The concern of the training staff, and often the formal budget reports of the training unit, is with measures of activity: training hours provided, training seats filled, numbers of programs delivered, and so forth. Almost never are long-range results of training assessed, nor are training staff terribly concerned with them.

The Trainee Satisfaction Spiral. As casual observation shows and recent research (Gutek, 1988; Smith, 1984; Brandenburg, 1988) verifies, virtually all formal training in today's organizations is concluded with the ubiquitous end-of-session trainee satisfaction survey. This practice is, in many ways, quite sensible. Trainee feedback is, of course, a vital component of training evaluation (that is what Kirkpatrick's 1977 model refers to as "reaction" evaluation); trainee satisfaction clearly reflects some dimensions of relevance to learning, and trainees can often make very good suggestions for revision. Further, the end-of-session survey practice demonstrates a sensitivity to principles of accountability and trainee interests. Thus, if one sets aside some very obvious psychometric and psychological deficiencies (the tendency toward leniency, halo effect, and so forth), the end-of-session survey has some redeeming virtues.

But the trainee satisfaction survey often reflects a deep confusion about who is the legitimate customer of training. In the broad scheme of the organization, training is a service activity designed to address the needs of the organization, and thus the true "customers" of training are upper-level management. Their satisfaction with training stems more legitimately from the extent to which it has helped the organization profit and gain competitive advantage than from the extent to which it has entertained and placated employees.

My observations in dozens of corporate settings are that training professionals have become overly obsessed with customer satisfaction (where customers are mistakenly viewed as the trainees). Trainers, especially those whose organizational performance appraisals include trainee satisfaction measures, tend to overemphasize the performance aspects of their roles. Training sessions are becoming increasingly glitzy and glossy stage productions; trainee expectations for entertainment and polished performances push the stakes ever higher. The trainee satisfaction survey, I fear, represents a glaring example of the more general measurement principle that measurement drives, as well as reflects, performance; what gets counted must, we believe, count.

Training-Inherent Problems. Whereas the phenomena and trends I have reviewed above are emerging with the growth of training, training also is plagued by some inherently problematic characteristics. Some of the characteristics that evaluators must be especially sensitive to are the following:

1. Skills, knowledge, and superficial attitudes and beliefs (SKA) are the only things that training can change. Yet these SKAs are only a part of the larger human performance puzzle, as many researchers and writers have noted (see especially Gilbert, 1978). When training does show results, and when it does not, it is impossible to attribute complete credit or blame to training. The eventual worth of training as manifested in organizational impact will always be a function of many nontraining factors, such as compensation, job design, reward structures, tools, and information.

2. Some of the results of training may not be evident for long periods of time. When training is directed at immediate job performance problems, immediate results can be expected. But, when training is a part of a large effort to transform the culture of an organization, as with, for example, the Ford Motor Company's recent efforts to upgrade quality, results emerge slowly over many years.

3. Training has a number of indirect benefits, which additionally will be differentially valued by different elements of an organization. Some trainees attending a job skill program, for example, may not gain any of the intended skills; but these same trainees may become more motivated than before by the sense that the company cares about them and thus become more loyal employees who tend to work more diligently and to resist recruitment efforts by other organizations. A mandatory corporate supervisory-preparation program may be valued very little by line managers who see only low quarterly productivity, but strongly revered by corporate managers who aim to enhance the long-term growth of the company. Training has multiple results—some related to productivity, others to staff benefits and growth of human capital—that will benefit different dimensions of the organization in different ways.

4. Training often has a history of abuse and absence of impact. In

virtually every organization where I have inquired, I find people who can tell me training "horror" stories. Some of the more common (and true) folktales include (1) the training session someone attended that had no relevance whatsoever to his or her job; (2) the trainer who, in painfully obvious ways, had no expertise at all in the purported training topic; (3) the training that, upon its closing, won rave reviews, but no one remembered anything about it the following week; and (4) the trainee who learned a nifty new work method only to discover, back on the job, that no one really wanted things done that way. The result of all these negative experiences is, of course, that virtually anyone with some organizational experience will look at training with at least a partially jaundiced eye.

The Future of Training Evaluation

The proper role of evaluation is, I believe, to help counter the many problems and forces acting against the effectiveness of training that I have reviewed and discussed thus far. The services of a strong training function are vitally important to virtually any large organization. Yet, evaluation business-as-usual will not help to position training as the important business partner it could and should be. I first note two historically prevalent foci of evaluation and then outline an agenda for future evaluation efforts.

Misplaced Efforts

A casual review of the evaluation literature, or more formal efforts such as reported by Brandenburg (1988), indicates that evaluation has largely concerned itself with either (1) improving the educational quality of training or (2) somehow "proving" that training can make a difference. The improvement efforts are aimed at increasing and assessing either or both trainee satisfaction and trainee learning, or they are aimed at comparing the learning utility of alternative training programs, such as an instructor-led workshop versus a self-instructional program. So-called proof efforts attempt to gather quantifiable information that will somehow demonstrate that training can, or did, make a noticeable difference. Both such efforts are, I think largely wasted.

The Proof Fallacy. In the case of the proof efforts, evaluators of training have employed methods based on experimental design to assess whether training produces noticeable and statistically significant results. Such studies are of interest to researchers and have their place in research on training and development. At best, the purposes of such studies are, however, of little practical utility in an applied organizational setting. At worst, they are detrimental, for they divert evaluation resources from more useful applications, and they misrepresent the purposes and function of training.

The major difficulty with the proof efforts is their focus on parceling out the contribution that training makes to a specific or general organizational function. Many trainers and evaluators have occupied themselves, and spent considerable resources, in pursuit of evaluative data that will show what portion of a result, increased sales, for instance, can be attributed to training.

Consider, for example, a company I once worked with that had invested huge sums of money in new computer systems and new operations procedures. Training was an integral and necessary element of this large-scale organizational change effort, as the major portion of nearly every employee's job was being changed.

Evaluation of this training showed that it worked very well: trainees mastered new skills efficiently, and follow-up evaluation showed that they used them effectively, though continued supervisory support was vital. Further, organizational performance data related to each job (sales conversions, error rates, customer satisfaction, and so forth) showed that the overall organizational change was working quite successfully. Where performance difficulties were encountered, the evaluation data clearly indicated that factors other than training deficiencies (malfunctioning equipment, inadequate management procedures, and misjudged work loads, for example) were the major culprits. In this case, training was clearly and vitally needed as an integral part of the organization's transition to new technology. And it had fulfilled its role. No evaluation was wanted or needed to decide whether training was necessary. Instead, the most important evaluation questions were as follows: What skills and knowledge are most needed? What kind of training is most likely to work best? How well is the training working, and what problems are cropping up? And finally, what follow-up training needs are emerging among all the key job roles?

In sum, training is often a necessary given because it is vital to the successful implementation of organizational goals. In such instances, it is the role of evaluation to ensure that training makes the most effective and efficient contribution possible, rather than to question how much contribution it alone has made. To make an analogy to the automobile industry, it would be ludicrous and wasteful for the engine production function to "evaluate" the size and significance of the engine's contribution as compared to, say, the contribution of the chassis. What is crucial is that engine and chassis builders work well together, and that the components they produce are effective, efficiently made, and complement one another in the final product. Where training is truly needed and reasonably well designed and delivered, it will automatically make a difference. Where training is not truly needed, it will not make any difference regardless of how well it is done. In either case, a solid needs assessment, not some narrowly construed, after the fact, experimental-design-based evaluation, is needed first. Then, subsequent evaluation should be dedicated to the effective and efficient operation and contribution of training to organizational goals.

Fixing Most What is Broken Least. In the case of improvement, training is already typically very well done in most organizations; it uses good technology, and trainees like it about as much as one could expect, if not even more than we would want. Where training is very badly performed, it does not take much evaluation to discover weaknesses, and training technology is such that "fixes" are readily available.

Where training is already reasonably well designed and delivered (and I suspect this is the case in most large organizations), further enhancements are not likely to yield more than marginal results. Evaluation is far more likely to yield high returns (where evaluation return is defined as information that can be used to add value to the training function) when it is applied elsewhere in the training process.

Imagine that three "zones" constitute the overall training process: Zone 1: before training, Zone 2: during training, and Zone 3: after training. Zone 1 represents those things done to "get ready" for training, such as determining needs, building readiness, gaining management support, identifying obstacles to performance and transfer of training, setting objectives, creating a project plan, and so forth. Zone 2 includes conducting the training, teaching trainees, leading training, measuring learning, and so on. Zone 3 is composed of trainees attempting to use the training and supervisors interacting with newly trained employees, identifying and overcoming emerging barriers to training utilization, identifying emerging training needs, and so forth. Each zone is characterized by certain decisions and concerns:

Zone 1. What is the problem? Who would benefit most from training? What is the payoff of training likely to be? Whose support is needed to make the training work? What organization and individual performance barriers will impede training results? What kind of training works best?

Zone 2. How well do trainees learn? How much do trainees like the training? What learning activities are working best? How is the training going? What about the training should be changed? How well is the instructor doing?

Zone 3. How much of the training is being used? Who is using the training the best? Why is the training not being used? What is happening that is undermining the training? How is the training being supported? What kind of benefits result from the training?

The greatest returns on the training investment come not from intervening in Zone 2 but rather from making activities effective in Zones 1 and 3. I recently was involved with a training program in formal decision making and problem analysis (an expensive vendor-supplied package) in a leading Fortune 500 corporation. Evaluation of this session showed that (1) almost 100 percent of the trainees learned the content to criterion skill and knowledge levels; (2) only 20 percent indicated a willingness and interest in using the learned procedures on the job (most said that their jobs were much simpler than trained for and the procedures learned were too complex); and (3) less than 9 percent indicated in a three-month follow-up that they had made any use at all of the training. Despite the 100 percent learning rate, about 90 percent of the training investment was wasted. In short, had the company only trained about 20 percent of the employees in the first place (those who really needed and could use the training) and then aggressively supported those few trainees in using the training, they could have achieved a 100 percent application rate at a dramatically decreased training cost. However, no amount of improvement in the training event itself would have yielded any improvement in training return.

Most training professionals are reasonably well trained in instructional design and methods, or what Swanson (1987) has defined as the "psychological" dimension of training. Futher, most of the training literature focuses on instructional design, instructor skills, evaluation of learning, and so forth. Where trainers are typically far less skilled and prepared is in the role of "change agent." The result, of course, is that those aspects of the training function that deal with preparing for change, and with helping the organization adapt to change and continuously improve performance, are paid the least attention. Help, then, is needed most in those areas where most evaluation is paying the least attention.

Effective evaluation efforts aimed at Zones 1 and 3 are likely to lead to vast improvements in the impact of training. Evaluation investment in Zone 1, such as evaluating and forecasting potential returns, assessing alternative plans, identifying high-performance trainees, determining trainee readiness, and assessing individual and organizational impediments, would help trainers increase the probability of return on the training investment. Likewise, conducting highly focused follow-up evaluations of training usage, managerial support, usage failures and opportunities, and so forth, would not only increase the immediate training return but also help trainers develop effective policies and procedures for future training efforts.

Promising Directions

I propose here a number of directions that I believe evaluation of training should follow into the next decade. Each of these is based on emerging trends and new approaches, and each is intended to counter the negative phenomena and practices discussed earlier. None of these new directions requires new evaluation technology or measurement techniques; the tools are already in place. What these new directions require is new applications, new purposes, new evaluation questions, and new alliances and involvements.

While I list and briefly discuss each of these new directions separately, it should be understood that they are interrelated and that each alone is insufficient. A focus on needs-driven planning, for example, entails close ties to management, which likewise relies on a customer service orientation.

Shift to Needs-Driven Versus Program-Driven Training. It is the results of training and the application of new skills, knowledge, and attitudes that organizations need, not training programs. Evaluation, by focusing on training results and related organizational factors (management support, for example) that impinge on results, can help the training culture become more results conscious. In essence, this requires that training evaluators pay more attention to needs assessment and to follow-up of training application and impediments.

The following are critical evaluation questions: (1) What training goals, current and future, will best serve business needs and strategic priorities? (2) To what extent are current training results sufficient to support business needs? (3) What additional training would best serve business needs? (4) What revisions and improvements to existing training programs (including deletions) would best serve business needs?

These questions clearly indicate an element of professional judgment, and they likewise indicate a need for detailed understanding of an organization's strategy, goals, problems, and business priorities. Trainers and evaluators need, then, close ties to top management, and they must make continued efforts to review training programs in light of organizational goals and strategy. Because strategy and goals are dynamic, these efforts must be ongoing. To this end, I have sometimes helped companies establish management review panels that meet regularly to consider training-program accomplishments and content in relation to the organization's needs and priorities.

Finally, a shift to a needs-driven orientation should, in most cases, seek to reduce training "inventory." Just as many manufacturing operations have found it more productive to use just-in-time inventory approaches, so too a training unit can benefit from reducing its emphasis on maintenance of a heavy curriculum inventory, increasing its investment in needs assessment and follow-up services, and providing highly tailored and responsive training as needed.

Emphasize Customer Service. Training must be designed and delivered to meet the needs of customers—the top management personnel of organizations. Customer service efforts in any industry require ongoing contact with customers, understanding of customer needs and expectations (which, it should be noted, are not always identical), and appreciation for the context within which customers use products and services.

A focus on customer service entails several evaluation efforts. These should include measures (surveys, for example) of customer satisfaction with and expectations about the services received, studies of customer needs and priorities, research into customers' problems and particular issues of importance, and other efforts to "get to know" customers and their contexts.

Create Close Ties with Management. Evaluation can serve to educate management about training, and it can help to build management commitment. Regular training-evaluation reports, specially designed to catch and maintain management interest, can help managers understand the goals, achievements, and shortcomings of training. Not only does such reporting help build positive, open relationships, but managers become better educated consumers of training, a process that creates more realistic expectations and more sympathetic acceptance of inevitable training problems and issues.

Building commitment for training involves more than getting management to support training and to give trainers access to organizational effectiveness data. Such resources and access are crucial, of course. But equally, if not more, important is a commitment from management to share accountability for the results of training. Evaluation should not only be designed to assess and report the results of training. It should also be focused on the related dimensions that interact with training effects, such as supervisory support and rewards and incentives. These related factors are typically beyond the administrative control of training managers, but they nonetheless impinge on the success of training as it relates to organizational performance.

Focus Evaluation on Specific Training "Targets." As noted earlier, training has multiple effects, and different audiences (managers, trainees, and support personnel, for example) have different expectations for and needs related to any given training program. Although this potential for multiple results makes training valuable, it also contributes to an environment where there can be confusion about accountability for results, as well as uncertainty about which results to expect in the first place. Evaluators can serve training value better when they help identify highly specific objectives for training, especially in the areas (or "zones") related to the establishment of preconditions for training and to the subsequent application of learning results.

I worked recently with a statewide banking company that had embarked on a strategic transformation of their business to increase orientation toward sales and customer service. As a part of their transformation, they had purchased a large training program to teach both selling and sales-support skills to each employee. Initial evaluation showed that the program was popular, but there was virtually no change in the employees' on-the-job behaviors. Further inquiry revealed that there was widespread uncertainty about just how and when to use the new behaviors, and that managers were at the same time unable to provide effective coaching. As evaluators, we helped the bank define specific behavior goals for each bank job that, if achieved, would lead to strategic business success. Then, we constructed measures of organizational performance (increased sales, for example) that could be specifically tied to related sets of job behaviors. Data about behavior frequency and achievement of performance objectives were included in the training, and trainees were also trained to collect further data about their attempts to use the training. As a result, the training incorporated increasingly more specific examples and objectives (which facilitated learning, and thus confidence), and the training built awareness of and commitment to monitor and achieve the company's strategic goals.

The construction of evaluation targets and measures as a front-end activity is clearly time consuming and expensive, but the payoff is more than likely to be worthwhile. Such up-front analysis of expected returns, when targeted specifically (and individually, where possible), helps to (1) build awareness of and commitment to training and business goals; (2) clarify and negotiate multiple expectations; and (3) assure achievement of goals by focusing attention on the most critical results of training.

Use a Quality Control and Management Approach. The recent revolution in quality management (see, for example, Deming, 1986) has produced significant lessons for evaluation of training. Earlier approaches to quality control were based on inspection: get some people to build lots of products (cars, for example) and then get some other people to inspect them for quality and to throw away any rejects. The inspection approach is effective to the extent that it keeps poor quality products from going out the door, but it fosters lack of responsibility for quality production, and it creates increasing rework costs. In contrast, the current approaches aim to build quality into the product by giving workers the tools for measuring and the responsibility for achieving quality during each production step. These approaches have been very successful, obviating the need for inspection and creating significant productivity increases.

The applications for training are relatively obvious. Each step of the training process—needs identification, planning, designing, delivery, and follow-up—should be analyzed, and quality criteria for each step identified. Once this is done, quality training becomes a matter of giving training practitioners at each step the tools and responsibility for assessing and maintaining their own quality levels.

Create a Developmental Environment. I have often told training audiences that they best serve their customers when they view every training program as a "pilot." My message here springs from three facts of organizational life. The first fact is related to the likelihood that no training program, however well designed and operated, is error free. Evaluation is likely, then, to virtually always produce information useful for revision.

The second fact is more significant than the first: Every training target is a moving target. By the time training is designed and implemented, the organizational factors and context from which the training needs the were derived will have changed. Thus, the program that starts small, serving only a relatively minor portion of the total needs audience, can be managed more effectively to meet those needs and will provide a real-life laboratory to study and refine the results of training.

The third fact is that training needs have highly localized variations, despite being generically widespread. It may be, for example, that a company has a need to train all of its managers in how to manage and facilitate change. But the specific change-management needs of the sales-training division are likely to be different from the specific needs of the research division, or those of the personnel department. Close evaluation and reporting within, rather than across, these different application areas thus better serve customers and create more opportunities for training-program development and revision.

In sum, training is best delivered in an iterative, cyclical fashion characterized by close and frequent evaluation. Such an approach enables highly responsive training-content variations within a program and permits successive trial and refinement cycles.

Demonstrate a Commitment to Training Alternatives. Training is expensive. Because most organizations track only direct instructional costs of training, failing to include trainee time and lost production as a cost, it is many times more expensive than typically accounted for.

Probably because training has become a commonplace fixture in most organizations, it is frequently resorted to when cheaper alternatives would work equally well, if not better. Not too long ago I worked with a client organization that requested training for all of its forklift drivers; the reported (and thoroughly documented) problem was that drivers did not know the warehouse arrangement well enough and thus spent too much time driving around and searching for products. The solution implemented was not training but rather reproduced copies (modified weekly) of warehouse maps that were pasted onto each lift truck's dashboard. These maps included highlighted routes, derived from data we collected about the sequence in which commonly sought products could be most efficiently picked up.

Evaluation of training should include evaluation of alternatives to training as a regular component of front-end analysis. Further, follow-up evaluation of trainees should aim to seek out opportunities for training alternatives, such as job redesign or job aids. Often the first "wave" of trainees will figure out how to do a job better than specified by the job designers, and thus subsequent training needs can be reduced or even eliminated where simpler procedures or job aids can be employed.

Summary

Training has come a long way in the past few decades. It is far more widespread and richly endowed than ever before. The need for effective training is probably greater than ever before, as the world enters a new and highly competitive global market where technological advances come ever more rapidly to a shrinking, and thus more static, labor force. Today's and tomorrow's workplaces now require and will continue to require most old (and young) dogs to learn many new tricks.

Training is an organizational imperative. It is often vitally needed, though there may be considerable confusion about the nature and scope of training needs. The role of evaluation is to ensure that training resources are effectively deployed to best serve strategic needs, and that training operations deliver optimum value. Fulfillment of this agenda, however, will require significant changes in the thinking of both trainers and evaluators. It will require not evaluation responsive to yesterday's needs but rather evaluation that is proactive and directive—evaluation that will drive training to new levels of added value and to greater contributions to business performance.

References

Albrecht, K., and Zemke, B. *Service America!: Doing Business in the New Economy.* Homewood, Ill.: Dow Jones-Irwin, 1985.

Brandenburg, D. C. "The Status of Training Evaluation: An Update." Paper presented at the National Society for Performance and Instruction Conference, Washington, D.C., 1988.

Carnevale, A. P. "The Learning Enterprise." *Training and Development Journal,* 1986, *45,* 18-26.

Deming, E. W. *Out of the Crisis.* Cambridge, Mass.: Massachusetts Institute of Technology, Center for Advanced Engineering Study, 1986.

Desatnick, R. L. *Managing to Keep the Customer: How to Achieve and Maintain Superior Customer Service Throughout the Organization.* San Francisco: Jossey-Bass, 1987.

Eurich, N. P. *Corporate Classrooms.* Princeton, N.J.: Princeton University Press, 1985.

Gilbert, T. F. *Human Competence: Engineering Worthy Performance.* New York: McGraw-Hill, 1978.

Gutek, S. P. "Training-Program Evaluation: An Investigation of Perceptions and Practices in Nonmanufacturing Business Organizations." Unpublished doctoral dissertation, Western Michigan University, 1988.

Hayes, G. E. *Quality & Productivity: The New Challenge.* Wheaton, Ill.: Hitchcock, 1985.

Kirkpatrick, D. L. "Evaluating Training Programs: Evidence vs. Proof." *Training and Development Journal,* 1977, *31,* 9-12.

Peters, T. J. *A Passion for Excellence: The Leadership Difference.* New York: Random House, 1985.

Robinson, D. G., and Robinson, J. C. *Training for Impact: How to Link Training to Business Needs and Measure the Results.* San Francisco: Jossey-Bass, 1989.

Smith, M. E. "Trends in Training Evaluation." Paper presented at the National Society for Performance and Instruction Conference, Atlanta, Georgia, April 24, 1984.

Swanson, R. A. "Industrial Training." In W. H. Mitzel (ed.), *Encyclopedia of Educational Research.* 5th ed. New York: Macmillan, 1982.

Swanson, R. A. "Training Technology System: A Method for Identifying and Solving Training Problems in Industry and Business." *Journal of Industrial Teacher Education,* 1987, *24* (4), 7-17.

Tichy, N. M. *The Transformational Leader.* New York: Wiley, 1986.

Robert O. Brinkerhoff is professor of Educational Leadership at Western Michigan University, where he coordinates graduate programs in training and development. He holds a doctorate in program evaluation from the University of Virginia and provides consultation in training and evaluation to a number of large corporations in the United States, Africa, Australia, and Europe.

Training programs and results are strengthened when evaluators take care to ask the right questions.

Evaluating the Merit and Worth of Sales Training: Asking the Right Questions

Dale M. Brethower

Sales training has become increasingly important in recent years as several industries have experienced serious problems recruiting needed salespeople. In addition, it has become increasingly difficult to train and retain salespeople as the technological complexity of products and services has increased.

Sales training has become strategically important, not only to commercial organizations but also to evaluators as we attempt to develop the discipline and extend it to new applications. Basic concepts of educational and program evaluation apply quite directly to sales training. In addition, the evaluation lessons learned through helping sales trainers deal with some of the unique challenges facing them can help evaluators discover how to deal with challenges in other areas.

In the following discussion, I illustrate, first, how basic concepts of evaluation apply in the sales-training arena: People make evaluative statements, whether or not the evaluation is done carefully and well; personal biases and beliefs about the purposes of sales training influence judgments about whether (sales) training is good or bad. After examining the bases of evaluative statements, I turn to the practical tasks of getting agreement on the criteria for evaluation and using evaluation questions to focus evaluative effort on issues of worth (What does sales training contribute to the organization?) and merit (How good is the sales training?). Then I attempt to show that sales training is a cyclic process that can be evaluated through cyclic evaluation processes. I also argue that the evaluation process can be technically and politically imperiled by asking the wrong evaluation questions.

Evaluative Statements About Sales Training

Each of the following statements reflects evaluation of sales training:

I learned a new technique that enabled me to close three tough sales that I'd been working on for weeks.
Our sales training is world class!
You should have been there! The service at the resort was marvelous! I went home ready to go out and do battle for another couple of months.
The speaker was terrible! He couldn't sell dry firewood to wet campers.
The VP might have had something to say about the new product, but he was so boring we all slept through it.
The sessions were the same old thing, but I got some good pointers from some of the people there.
I don't know why you have to hold your sales training sessions at expensive resorts; nobody else in the company gets to throw money around like that.
Our sales training stinks. They don't give us a decent budget.

Evaluative statements of this sort are made by people with a stake in the sales training, for example, participants in training sessions, vice presidents of sales, sales trainers, and budget officers. Each stakeholder evaluates sales training from her or his organizational perspective and personal biases. The evaluative statements illustrate a natural human tendency: We are natural evaluators of our experiences. We evaluate restaurants, television commercials, movies, music, sex appeal, talk show hosts, bosses, teachers, wine coolers, cars, cake recipes, and sales training. Every organization that does sales training evaluates it, whether consciously or not, for better or for worse.

Primitive Evaluative Statements. Evaluation, in its most primitive form, is simply a gut level reaction, as people respond to each experience positively, negatively, or neutrally. Evaluative reactions are conditioned by past history, values, self-interests, perceptions of reality, and sometimes by careful consideration of the facts. But people always evaluate. Furthermore, sales-training stakeholders usually believe the evaluative statements they make and sometimes act upon them, encouraging other people to attend or be attentive, to stay away, to have high or low expectations, or to cut or add to the sales-training budget.

Consequences of Evaluative Statements. Stakeholders make evaluative statements about sales training; furthermore, their evaluations have practical consequences for sales training. If participants come in expecting inspirational speakers and get dull product knowledge; if participants come in expecting important product knowledge and get motivational hype; if a vice president expects world-class training and gets good training but with amateurish training materials; if a budget officer expects an austere budget proposal and gets one that would support world-class training; if any of these expectations are not met, there will be specific consequences for sales training.

Evaluating proactively is safer than being at the mercy of primitive evaluation. The collection of evaluation data helps sales trainers identify existing expectations and live up to and maintain the constructive ones. The collection of evaluation data also helps sales trainers correct inaccurate evaluative statements and identify and correct problems contributing to negative statements.

Beliefs Influencing Evaluative Statements. The statements we would like to hear (or make) about sales training are determined by our ideas about what sales training should accomplish in a specific organization. For example, if we believe the primary mission of sales training is to maintain the morale of the sales force, we would want to hear "You shoulda been there . . . ." If we believe the primary mission of sales training is to get experienced salespeople together to share experiences, we would be pleased to hear "I got some good pointers from some of the people there."

The following are statements that sales trainers have made to me over the years about sales training. The implied sales-training mission is provided in parentheses:

> We believe that salespeople are professionals. We serve as a resource to them to keep up their skills and to develop new skills. (The mission is knowledge and skill development.)
> Sales training is primarily motivational. We bring people in to pump them up and send them out again all fired up and ready to sell. (The mission is motivation.)
> There is a lot of turnover among our salespeople. Our products keep changing, too. We have to keep training all the time just to give new people the basics about our products and procedures. (The mission is managing change in salespersons and products.)
> Our industry is tough on salespeople. We have to bring them in every

once in a while for rest and relaxation so they don't burn out. We give them some motivational speeches and the new sales brochures and things, but if we didn't do it at a nice resort where they can relax, we would lose even more than we do. (The mission is providing R and R to retain salespeople.)

Our sales training is results oriented. If there is a new product or new marketing tactic, we kick it off with sales training. Or if we are in a sales slump, we bring people in to analyze the problem and get everybody to do what they need to pull us out of it. We want a direct connection to the bottom line. (The mission is to produce specific sales results.)

Clearly, these different beliefs about the primary mission of sales training influence what stakeholders look for in sales training. Each implied mission has merit that we should consider as we establish formal evaluation criteria.

Evaluation Criteria

Stakeholders' beliefs about the missions of sales training and their related beliefs about what "good sales training" is determine their criteria for deciding whether an evaluative statement is good, bad, or neutral and for deciding what action to take based on the evaluation. For example, the person who believes that the mission of sales training is to help achieve a good sales dollar-to-sales cost ratio would be quite concerned about the budget officer's comments and might seek a reduction in costs; on the other hand, the person who believes that the mission is to entertain and keep sales people on board would just explain the facts of life to the budget officer and alert the vice president of sales to the possibility of another misguided attack on the budget by the bean counters.

But if peoples' personal beliefs and biases determine what they consider to be good, how do we get consensus on what good sales training is? The question is central to the evaluation of sales training. It must be faced directly if we are to move forward in the profession.

Getting Agreement on Criteria. One of the most important parts of evaluation is the establishment of evaluation criteria (compare Brinkerhoff, Brethower, Hluchyj, and Nowakowski, 1983b). Formal evaluation involves making evaluative statements based on the best available evidence and judged in terms of shared and defensible evaluation criteria: What criteria do we use to consider something good? What are the criteria or standards by which we judge sales training?

The sales trainer who attempts to develop sales training without knowing the criteria is in the same position as the automotive supplier who sets out to design and manufacture a part for a car without having design specifications. Ironically, managers who would not dream of asking a design engineer to do such a foolish thing, ask it of sales trainers routinely: "Build a training program to help us out of this sales slump!" "What sort of training do you need?" "I don't know! You're the sales-training expert. You decide, but I don't want you bothering my people with questions."

There is, however, a sense in which the managers are right: the sales trainer is the expert and should work up the design specifications and get a sign-off on them. That can be done effectively by integrating evaluation into the sales-training process. It is possible to get specific questions answered during a needs assessment phase, thereby (1) getting agreement on what the sales-training program is supposed to accomplish and (2) providing a basis for design specifications that are approved during the design phase of the training cycle.

Criteria for Worth of Sales Training. All other things being equal, competent sales training will produce economic benefits. Sales training should be related, by logic and operational practice, to business strategy. But it is not obvious to most people just how economic and other benefits of sales training can be measured.

Suppose, for example, that everyone in Acme Baby Care Products agrees that sales training should be results-directed and contribute to the bottom line. Sales trainers would want to be able to say, "Our sales training contributed significantly to the unprecedented growth in sales of our new improved line of biodegradable diapers." But it is much easier to say it than to prove it.

Sometimes the bottom-line claim would be accepted just because everyone is feeling good about a success. But what about Acme's vice-president of marketing who just bet a million dollars of the company's money and her job on a television campaign? She might be reluctant to give all the credit to the director of sales training. So too might the people in R & D who are inclined to believe that good products sell themselves.

It is occasionally possible to demonstrate that sales training made a significant dollar contribution. Events can fall into place so that a controlled experiment occurs by accident. For example, the TV campaign and all the rest of the kick-off campaign might occur nationally in June, but sales training may be delayed in two of four regions. If the sales training occurred in September in one region and in October in the other, and there were accompanying jumps in sales in both regions, then the statement "Our sales training contributed significantly. . . ." would have some credibility. Even so, there is a better way to evaluate the contribution of sales training.

The better way is to assure the relevance to specific business results and then evaluate the quality of training. Relevance is established during a properly conducted assessment and can be documented during needs assessment. Showing that the business results are attained and demonstrating the high quality of the entire training cycle are sufficient to show that the sales training did its job. Furthermore, such evaluation can be done on a routine basis and still cost less than the expensive mistakes that can result from inadequate needs assessment.

Criteria for Quality and Merit of Sales Training. Significant economic benefits are achieved through the cooperative competence of many. For example, production is useless without sales, and vice versa; similarly, accounting and personnel and data processing are necessary but only in relationship to the rest of the business. One business activity cannot properly take credit for the sustained success that results from the combined efforts of many. It is simply wrongheaded to ask, "Did the sales-training program result in an increase in sales?" or "Did the new accounting procedures result in significant cost savings?" We need to know if sales increased and if the program was competently done; however, we do not need to establish a causal relationship between the sales training (one of many functions involved) and the sales increase.

Criteria for quality are established by convention, by consensus, and by optimization among competing criteria. When we design and build quality into an automobile, we simply agree on a set of specifications and build to those specifications. The specifications should be carefully negotiated among market researchers, automotive engineers, and manufacturing experts. The specifications might not be perfect from anyone's perspective, but taken as a whole, they enable people to build quality products. A quality product is, by definition, one that meets quality specifications. Similarly, a high-quality sales-training program is, by definition, one that meets quality specifications.

An obvious pitfall in this approach to quality is that the quality specifications or standards are sometimes weak or skewed. For example, if the automotive engineers get their way too much, the company will produce high-quality (and high-priced) cars that customers will not buy. Or, if the marketing people get their way too much, the company will produce cars that look good to customers but are not well engineered.

The fact that quality standards sometimes get skewed does not mean that we should abandon quality standards but rather that we should redouble our efforts to establish workable quality standards that are not skewed. Quality assurance procedures have a long history of success and can be applied to the establishment of high-quality training (compare Ruyle, 1989). It is simply a matter of doing the work necessary to hammer out specifications, producing in accordance with those specifications, and (with time and experience) improving the specifications.

Operations auditing and management auditing use a similar approach. The management or operations auditor asks a lot of questions about whatever is being audited. The questions are about important variables, that is, variables likely to influence the quality of performance of the operation being audited. An experienced auditor can analyze the answers and make reasonable suggestions for improvement. The process of evaluating sales training works in the same way. The evaluator asks questions relevant to important dimensions of quality of various parts of the training cycle and then applies quality specifications to the answers to arrive at conclusions about quality. We say that a training program that meets agreed-upon quality standards meet *merit* standards, following Michael Scriven's (1981) well-known usage. Scriven's language deals with the fact that a well-designed and well-executed training program might fail to be *worth* anything owing to unforeseeable factors beyond the control of trainers. Consequently, it is useful to have a way of saying, "The operation was a success but the patient died." For example, "The training program was high in merit but low in worth because of an overwhelmingly successful marketing program by one of our competitors."

Evaluation Questions

The evaluation of sales training, like operations auditing, involves the tenacious pursuit of answers to important questions. Some of the questions are primarily business questions and relate directly to worth, for example, "What increases in revenues, decreases in costs, or better strategic positioning can we reliably attain through sales training?" Other questions are primarily training questions and relate to professional standards of merit, for example, "Do needs assessment procedures clearly identify the knowledge, skills, and work habits people need to develop through training?" Answers to the business questions tell us what training is worth to a specific organization at a specific time; answers to the quality/merit questions tell us whether the training is competently performed.

Business-worth and training-merit questions must be answered if sound decisions are to be made about sales training in today's competitive business environment. The following material is offered to illustrate the questions of merit and worth, and to show why both types of questions are needed.

Evaluation Questions: Worth of Sales Training. The following is the overall or summary evaluation question for the worth of sales training: What is the overall cost, what are the economic or strategic benefits, and do the benefits outweigh the costs?

To get into a position to answer this large question, we must answer many smaller ones. The following are some of the smaller questions related to the worth of sales training: What are the business results we need to achieve? How can sales training contribute to strategic business objectives? What are the current trends in sales and market share for our major products and services? What are the strengths and weaknesses in current sales performance? Are some people or divisions performing at exceptionally high levels? Are some people or divisions performing at exceptionally low levels? How is our sales-training strategy related to the life-cycle stage of each of our major products and services? Do we emphasize prospecting relevant to new products, the price and quality of mature products, and the declining price and continued service for aging products? How is sales training related to promotional campaigns and pricing? Do we frequently achieve the business results we set out to achieve? Do the benefits usually outweigh the costs?

Some of these smaller questions should be answered in detail for each sales-training program. Others, answered periodically, will apply to all the sales training done within the period.

Evaluation Questions: Merit of Sales Training. A fundamental question of merit should support questions of worth: Is the sales-training function competently conducted in terms of an identified need, appropriate design and delivery, and achievement of desired learning outcomes that are related to desired business results?

There are many smaller questions that must be answered first in order to answer the major question of merit (compare Saint and Brethower, 1988). To see how these smaller questions can be answered in a practical and proactive way, we must examine the sales-training cycle and then the evaluation cycle.

Sales-Training Cycle. The systematic sales-training cycle described below is representative of training cycles recommended by experts in the field (Brinkerhoff, 1987; Greer, 1989; Hahne, 1987; Mirman, 1982a, 1982b; Sleezer and Swanson, 1989).

High-quality sales training operates in a cycle:

1. *Assessing needs.* This step involves determining who, if anyone, lacks knowledge, skill, or attitudes needed for current performance or strategic performance needs; determining precisely what knowledge, skill, or attitude deficiencies exist; and reporting to other parts of the organization when related organizational change needs are discovered.

2. *Designing sales training.* This step involves designing a training system that enables precisely the right people to acquire precisely the right knowledge, skills, or attitudes and coordinating the training-system design with other organizational activities and changes.

3. *Conducting sales training.* This step involves operating the training system to ensure that precisely the right people learn precisely the right things at precisely the right times; and coordinating the training with other organizational activities and changes.

4. *Supporting sales training.* This step involves ensuring that needed follow-up support is provided to help people use what was learned in

training; and coordinating the support with other organizational activities and changes.

5. *Recycling.* This step involves responding to new sales-training needs or organizational change needs that emerge as the sales training is designed, implemented, conducted, and supported; and coordinating the new work with other organizational activities and changes.

The sales-training cycle begins with a needs assessment, during which the program is aligned with business needs using procedures similar to those described by Rummler (1987). Once aligned, it is possible to establish design specifications and, thereby, quality criteria. The training program then operates in concert with other related business activities; recycling occurs to make the changes necessary to produce the desired business results. As the next section shows, the evaluation cycle supports the sales-training cycle.

Evaluation Cycle. Evaluation of sales training occurs during every part of the sales-training cycle, as shown below (compare Brinkerhoff, Brethower, Hluchyj, and Nowakowski, 1983a).

1. *Needs assessment* is essentially an evaluation activity that addresses these evaluation questions: What is not occurring that should? What is occurring that should not? What needs to be learned by whom?
2. *Design evaluation* addresses these evaluation questions: Is the training system being designed efficiently? Is the training-system design a good one?
3. *Implementation evaluation* addresses these evaluation questions: Is the training properly conducted? What problems are encountered?
4. *Outcome evaluation* addresses these evaluation questions: Do the learners learn? Do the learners like the training? What unexpected problems are encountered?
5. *Evaluation of business results* addresses these evaluation questions: Do people use what they learned? What organizational results are achieved? What unexpected results are achieved?

Integration of evaluation questions into the training cycle provides a guidance system for dealing with the difficult problems that sales trainers face. It is very important, therefore, to ask the right questions. While the examples above express many of the questions that should be asked, it is important to avoid the wrong questions.

Asking the Wrong Questions

The following types of questions should be avoided: causal questions, comparative questions, and faultfinding questions.

Causal Questions. When people want to relate sales training to bottom-line results (or when they want to avoid doing so), they have a pernicious tendency to focus on the question of causation. "Did sales training *cause* the gain in sales?" is simply the wrong question. We want to know about sales results, so "Are the desired results being attained?" is the question to attend to. More important, there is a more useful question for evaluating sales training: "Is our sales-training function competently run?" The competence question is more useful for several reasons: (1) It is usually possible to answer it, whereas it is rarely possible to answer the causal question. (2) The competence question can (and should) be asked and answered on an ongoing basis, whereas the causal question can be asked and answered only in the past tense. (3) The competence question can be divided into several answerable parts, and the answers to each part are worth knowing; for example, Do we do needs assessment well? Do we design sales-training systems effectively and efficiently? Are our sales-training programs well designed? Are our sales-training programs well run? Are our sales-training programs well received? Do people learn from our sales training? Do people use what they learn? (4) Coupled with the question of worth (Are we achieving the business results?), the competence question yields much of the data we need to manage the sales-training function effectively.

Comparative Questions. Comparative questions often appear to seek answers sufficient for all time. They are commonly in the form of "Which is better . . . ?" "Which is better, interactive video or programmed instruction?" "Which is better, training people before they go to the field or after?" "Who is better, instructor A or instructor B?" But each half of the comparison is likely to be "better" under specific circumstances. For example, instructor A might be better for sales training that involves selling to production engineers, and instructor B might be better for sales training that involves selling to commercial artists.

The ever-popular, comparative, "Which is better" question can be replaced by the question "Under what conditions should we use . . . ?" "Under what conditions should we use interactive video? Programmed instruction? Preservice training? In-service training? Instructor A? Instructor B?" The "Under what conditions" question gets at what people really want to know.

Faultfinding Questions. I find fault with faultfinding questions because of their tendency to lead to dead ends and repetition of failure. "Why don't the lights work? The fuse is blown. OK, replace the fuse." "Why are sales down in region four? The salespeople aren't doing their job. OK, replace the salespeople."

A second and potentially more serious fault with faultfinding questions is that faults are easy to find but reliable and lasting solutions are not. Instead of asking, "What's wrong with our sales training in region four?" we might ask, "How can we get better sales results in region four?" The latter question is hard to answer, but it identifies what we really need to know.

Political Problems. Causal, comparative, and faultfinding questions are the wrong questions not only technically but also from a purely political perspective. The faultfinding questions, for example, present problems that are all too familiar to evaluators. People sometimes call for evaluation when they want to undercut a rival in the organization. Bringing in an outsider makes the process appear objective, but the real purpose is to collect political ammunition, some of which can end up in the evaluator's foot. Even if the evaluator handles the situation with great care to avoid embarrassment of stakeholders, the fact remains that the evaluator has been manipulated into the position of being a "hired gun," which makes it less likely that the evaluator (or any evaluator) can function effectively in that organization in the future.

It is not necessary to engage in faultfinding to weed out bad programs. Farmers have known for years that killing weeds simply produces empty spots in fields. Weed resistant fields are obtained by carefully nurturing growth of desired crops.

Comparative questions result in political problems very similar to those that result from faultfinding questions. Which is better, method A or method B? If the answer is method B, the people responsible for method A may feel quite slighted and defensive, or they may go on the offensive, if that is their style. In my experience, proponents of method A are more likely to seek flaws in the evaluation design and redouble their commitment to method A than they are to enthusiastically embrace method B. Educational methods studies have routinely attempted, during the last fifty years, to compare two methods, but such comparative studies have been singularly unfruitful. (It is a little too soon to make a judgment about recent and more sophisticated research designs involving multivariate analyses, but I would hazard the guess that we will eventually conclude that such research serves more to cloud the political issues than to resolve them.)

Causal questions run afoul of some of the same political problems facing faultfinding and comparative questions. If one part of an organization claims credit for a business result, other parts can quite properly feel slighted. While the slight need not result in political reprisals, human being what it is, political reprisals might well occur.

Causal arguments can further muddy the political waters with respect to comparative questions and faultfinding questions. For example, if we show that a sales-training program is weak, the trainers can appropriately argue that the real cause of the fault is to be found elsewhere, for example, in the lack of budget, or the lack of management support, or the lack of proper qualifications in the people being hired these days, or . . . .

Fortunately, we do not need to create political problems for ourselves by continuing to ask the wrong questions. We do not need causal, comparative, or faultfinding questions because we can ask and answer questions of worth and merit: "Are we getting the business results?" and "Is the sales-training function operating competently?"

Business Issues and Sales Training

Sales training is not budgeted as a charitable contribution: Sales training should make a positive contribution to the organization (Feeney, Staelin, O'Brien, and Dickinson, 1982). The contribution can take a variety of forms, including improvements in morale, company image, sales volume, sales mix, and salesperson turnover rates. Other contributions are possible, for example, helping to reduce unwanted variability in production schedules, increasing the percentage of repeat customers, and developing executive skills. Sales training should contribute to the achievement of long-range organizational goals and to the handling of current and strategic business issues.

The task of management is to manage resources in response to external pressures and opportunities and to internal goals, needs, and capabilities. As conditions change, so too do management priorities. As priorities change, so too does the contribution needed from sales training. At one time there might be a need for more sales to generate revenue for a strategic initiative. At another time there might be a need for less sales of a product or service already being produced at maximum capacity and more need for sales of a new but slow selling product. At another time there might be a need for an effort to switch customers from one product line near the end of its life cycle to another product line at the beginning of its life cycle. The mission of the sales function is not simply to sell, sell, sell! It is also to support the strategic plan for marketing and for the business as a whole.

The sales-training mission is dictated by organizational needs and by sales-training capabilities. (It would be foolish to establish a mission not needed by the organization and foolish to establish a mission not achievable by the function to which it is assigned.) The quality standards for sales training are dictated by the mission and by state-of-the-art knowledge of the sales process, training and development, instructional psychology, and learning theory (see Resnick, 1981; Odiorne and Rummler, 1988; Glaser and Bassock, 1989). The quality standards describe criteria for judging how well the state-of-the-art knowledge is applied to the tasks necessary to fulfill the mission.

If a sales-training function attends to the questions of worth during needs assessment, the sales-training programs will be aimed in the right direction. If a sales-training function then develops its own standards of merit, the sales-training programs will have the guidance necessary to do the job. And if the sales-training function attends to questions of worth again in evaluating business results, the standards of merit will be validated. Designing and delivering programs according to carefully defined specifications can enable sales trainers to be confident about their contributions to the achievement of business results.

References

Brinkerhoff, R. O. *Achieving Results from Training: How to Evaluate Human Resource Development to Strengthen Programs and Increase Impact.* San Francisco: Jossey-Bass, 1987.

Brinkerhoff, R. O., Brethower, D. M., Hluchyj, T., and Nowakowski, J. R. *Program Evaluation: Design Manual.* Boston: Kluwer-Nijhoff, 1983a.

Brinkerhoff, R. O., Brethower, D. M., Hluchyj, T., and Nowakowski, J. R. *Program Evaluation: Sourcebook.* Boston: Kluwer-Nijhoff, 1983b.

Feeney, E. J., Staelin, J. R., O'Brien, R. M., and Dickinson, A. M. "Increasing Sales Performance Among Airline Reservation Personnel." In R. M. O'Brien, A. M. Dickinson, and M. P. Rosow (eds.), *Industrial Behavior Modification: A Management Handbook.* New York: Pergamon Press, 1982.

Glaser, R., and Bassock, M. "Learning Theory and the Study of Instruction." *Annual Review of Psychology,* 1989, *40,* 631-666.

Greer, M. "Managing Follow-up Evaluation." *Performance & Instruction,* 1989, *28* (5), 10-15.

Hahne, C. E. "Sales Training." In R. L. Craig (ed.), *Training and Development Handbook.* New York: McGraw-Hill, 1987.

Mirman, R. "Performance Management in Sales Organizations." In L. W. Fredericksen (ed.), *Handbook of Organizational Behavior Management.* New York: McGraw-Hill, 1982a.

Mirman, R. "Sales Management: An Effective Performance System." In R. M. O'Brien, A. M. Dickinson, and M. P. Rosow (eds.), *Industrial Behavior Modification: A Management Handbook.* New York: Pergamon Press, 1982b.

Odiorne, G. S., and Rummler, G. A. *Training and Development: A Guide for Professionals.* Chicago: Commerce Clearing House, 1988.

Resnick, L. B. "Instructional Psychology." *Annual Review of Psychology,* 1981, *32,* 659-704.

Rummler, G. A. "Determining Needs." In R. L. Craig (ed.), *Training and Development Handbook.* New York: McGraw-Hill, 1987.

Ruyle, K. E. "To Improve Training . . . Reduce Variation." *Performance & Instruction,* 1989, *28* (2), 9-16.

Saint, M., and Brethower, D. M. "Evaluation of Sales Training." *Executive Knowledgeworks Newsletter, Special Edition,* 1988, 1-14.

Scriven, M. S. *The Logic of Evaluation.* Pt. Reyes, Calif.: Edgepress, 1981.

Sleezer, C. M., and Swanson, R. A. "Is Your Training Department Out of Control?" *Performance & Instruction,* 1989, *28* (5), 22-26.

Dale M. Brethower teaches and consults in the fields of training and industrial psychology and is professor of psychology at Western Michigan University, Kalamazoo.

How the process of evaluating training programs can be used to build managers' interest and involvement in training.

Using Evaluation to Build Commitment to Training

Stephen Joel Gill

One often overlooked purpose for evaluating an organization's training and development programs is to strengthen management's commitment to training. The education of employees has a generally low priority in most organizations, in part, because managers are not invested in that aspect of the business. This chapter describes how the process of program evaluation can be used to build management support of the training and development function.

In many organizations training and development activities are not considered central to the business of the organization. Managers tolerate training because they view it as either a staff benefit or a means to remedy a skill deficit for particular employees. However, it is not considered critical to the successful operation of the business.

Traditionally, managers have not had a means of observing the impact and result of training and development activities. Separated from the training and development function, managers do not create measures to indicate the return-on-investment (ROI) of education as it relates to their

---

The author acknowledges the ideas of John A. Seeley and the editorial assistance of Irene LaPorte in the preparation of this chapter.

particular responsibilities within their respective organizations. Therefore, they have no awareness of what is achieved through enhancement of skills and knowledge.

This situation leads to managers placing less value on training and development programs than they do on other corporate functions. The education of employees is considered a cost to be contained; management does not put the time and resources into the training function that it does into the other activities of the organization. Minimum resources are allocated to this function, and the training budget is always at risk of being cut in times of budget restraint.

Recent acknowledgment of the skill deficiency of the American worker has made business aware that training can be critical to the success and, in some cases, the survival of the organization. Carnevale, Gainer, and Meltzer (1989, p. 7), in their report on basic skills in the workplace, observed that "America's inability to sustain competitive advantage argues for better basic skills among non-supervisory skill and craft employees. With better skills, this group can participate more effectively in those phases that need improvement. Upskilling is becoming more crucial as technical and economic changes increase companies' reliance on individuals and working teams who are directly responsible for the production and the sale of competitive products and services."

Also, "upskilling" is crucial for supervisory employees; training and development programs can have a profound impact on a company at all personnel levels. Bernhard and Ingols (1988, p. 41) wrote that "at their best, T & D programs are tools to communicate change, implement strategy, and knit the corporation together. At their worst, they can fragment a company and stunt its growth." Rather than a "cost to be contained," training and development should be considered an investment in the future of the total business, much like equipment, R & D, and marketing.

User-Focused Evaluation

Evaluation can play a vital role in making the training and development function responsive to the business of an organization by answering some key questions. Kirkpatrick (1975), in his now classic four-stage model of program evaluation, argues that the evaluation of training programs should try to answer four major questions: (1) Did trainees like it (reaction)? (2) Did trainees learn anything (learning)? (3) Did trainees use what they learned on the job (behavior)? and (4) Did the training have any tangible results for the organization (results)? And, there are some additional questions that the evaluation process can answer: Is this the training that the organization needs to help it achieve its goals? Did the training help the organization move closer to the achievement of its goals? The answers to all of these questions will help an organization clarify how training and development activities contribute to the success of the business.

But the question remains of how to get managers to view training and development as a tool for achieving the strategic goals of the company. One answer to this question is to involve them in the *process* of evaluation rather than only the *results* of evaluation. No manager will pay attention to the information or make use of the information unless he or she has had input in asking the question in the first place, in collecting the information, and in interpreting the meaning of the information. Therefore, the idea underlying user-focused evaluation is that those people who will be called on to implement the findings of the evaluation should be involved in the evaluation itself. This "user" involvement in the evaluation process is not new to the evaluation field (although it is not often followed). Patton (1978) described this kind of involvement as part of his "utilization-focused evaluation" and Alkin, Daillak, and White (1979) also discussed the important role of the evaluation user. However, user involvement is a new concept in the evaluation of training and development programs.

In the user-focused approach the process of evaluation becomes as important as the outcome. The assumption is that the engagement of those people who have a stake in the outcome of the evaluation will enhance the quality of the evaluation and increase the likelihood that the results of the evaluation will be used. Therefore, these stakeholders become a part of the evaluation team, are continually informed about the evaluation, and help the evaluator interpret the results.

In the corporate sector, trainers are not thought to have a critical or central role in the organization, and any evaluation they do is viewed as serving themselves, not the corporation. Therefore, any attempt to involve managers in the evaluation or planning of training is likely to be met with strong resistance from managers outside of the training function. Sales managers, finance managers, and plant managers generally do not see the need for their participation in evaluation and planning for the training department. The usefulness of these managers' roles will be difficult to discern in the beginning. However, as the evaluation progresses, the managers will see that the training function has a vital connection to the corporation's strategic business plans and will begin to see the necessity of their own involvement.

Stages of User Involvement

In the user-focused evaluation approach the key audiences for the evaluation are involved in the evaluation process. The evaluation is responsive to the organization's needs for information, but at the same time, the evaluation activities are not intrusive in the training and development activities. The evaluation procedures can be modified to fit the organization's needs at any point in time. Data should be accurate and credible and presented in a form that is useful to the planning and decision-making processes of the organization.

Comprehensive program evaluations can be characterized in terms of six major stages: (1) designing the evaluation, (2) collecting the evaluation data, (3) analyzing the data, (4) reporting the findings, (5) creating recommendations, and (6) implementing the recommendations. At each of these stages of the evaluation there are specific actions that the evaluator should take to involve managers in the evaluation process.

Design. The key element of this stage is gathering information from top management regarding the purposes and strategies of the evaluation. Managers will want to know about the nature of the training, the cost of the training, and its impact on employees. These concerns can be addressed through the evaluation. If managers think that they have been heard and that the evaluation will be responsive to their needs for information, they will begin to see the role that training plays in those issues that primarily concern them. For example, a sales managers may want to know why a course on time management has very little participation from salespeople. The evaluation could be designed to find the reason for this poor attendance.

An evaluation advisory group that includes the top-level managers from all departments should be created. This group serves to provide the training function with a forum in which to receive input from the people who must support the function if it is to be successful. Involvement can build ownership in the evaluation and, therefore, a commitment to use the findings for enhancing the impact of training and development. For example, the advisory group can identify the information that various departments need in order to know whether or not training programs are helping them achieve their business goals. This group's awareness of the culture and history of the organization can help the evaluator select the most appropriate methods for collecting evaluation data. Culture and history may suggest a questionnaire survey in one organization and face-to-face interviews in another.

Although for the evaluator this approach is time consuming and risky (that is, the evaluator gives up some control), the advisory group and other stakeholders should be involved in the development of data collection instruments. Only these managers can provide valuable assistance to an external evaluator who is not familiar with the culture of the organization. Their advice about who will be able to answer each question can be very helpful in planning for the use of the instruments. Participation in the advisory group increases involvement in, and therefore commitment to, the training and development process.

Data Collection. Top-level managers can be very important sources of data. What they think about a program, how they have used a program, or what they want from training for their employees are useful evaluation questions. Also, asking them questions sends the message to managers that their thoughts are important to the success of the program. The overt support of management can be essential to gaining the cooperation of other people who also are data sources.

Data Analysis. To build commitment to training, the evaluation must be responsive to management's questions. Therefore, the analysis of the data should be structured so that management's key questions are answered. If a key question is "What is the cost of training," the analysis should result both in a list of the direct and indirect costs as defined by participants as well as in a comparison of these costs to the benefits of the training, possibly, to the costs of similar programs in other organizations.

Once the data have been organized and the key findings identified, managers can be brought into the data interpretation process. These managers can provide unique insight based on their understanding of the total organization and of each department. Therefore, evaluators should interpret the data from the managers' points of view. This opportunity for the evaluator to bring stakeholders into the evaluation is a very important stage in building commitment. Evaluators should discuss the meaning of the findings with the advisory group.

Interpretation of the findings can be done in a workshop environment. The evaluator can structure the experience so that a systematic review of the data is followed by active, hands-on experience that facilitates involvement by everyone present. If the data are in a computer data base, workshop participants can be given access to computers so that they can further analyze the data during the workshop. For stakeholders, this can be an exciting experience that adds considerable value to the data.

Reporting. The time frame and method of reporting findings can be determined by the advisory group, too. The fastest way to render an evaluation useless and discourage involvement in future evaluation efforts is to report the findings at a time or in a manner that does not fit the needs of the key stakeholders in the organization. Therefore, the advisory group can help the evaluators plan for timely reporting of findings and plan the format and procedures for reporting. Where one stakeholder may want a full report with "bells and whistles" when all the results are in, another stakeholder may be making an important decision that will affect training in a particular department and hence may need some specific findings on a specific date.

Creating Recommendations. This is another critical point at which the evaluator can build management's commitment to training. Involve the advisory group and other key stakeholders (that is, those people who will have primary responsibility for implementing the recommendations) in the development of recommendations from the findings. There is a much greater likelihood of acceptance and implementation of the recommendations if the stakeholders feel a sense of ownership in what is being proposed than if they do not.

Implementing Recommendations. The real test of whether or not an evaluation has been useful in building management's commitment to training is the extent to which the information is used. Does the new awareness of the effectiveness of training and development programs lead to greater use of training as a tool for achieving the business goals of the organization? The answer to this question depends on the process of implementing the recommendations. The evaluator plays an important role in this process by helping managers plan for the implementation of the recommendations. A systematic action-planning process should be created that results in the identification of what is to happen, who is responsible for making it happen, how they will make it happen, when and where it will happen, and what resources are needed. This process also serves to increase management commitment by helping managers plan change that is very concrete and realizable. Organization-wide support for the recommendations may need to be built by disseminating the findings through managers to their supervisees.

At each stage of the evaluation process there are strategies that can be used to increase the likelihood that the organization's management will become involved in training. First, because of their early involvement in the evaluation design and planning, stakeholders develop a sense of ownership in the evaluation results, and, therefore, in the training process. Second, ongoing involvement of stakeholders increases awareness of training and development efforts and understanding of the importance of training to the organization. Third, giving stakeholders a role in the interpretation of data and the creation or recommendations increases the likelihood that managers will support changes in training and development programs. This is particularly critical if training is competing with other parts of the organization for a large piece of the budget pie.

Application of the Approach

The leaders of a large manufacturing company recognized a need to enhance training effectiveness throughout the corporation. This need led to a request for external evaluators to examine the current training and development programs and to analyze the educational needs of all employee groups, including senior management, mid-level managers, and employees in the divisions of operations, sales, product development, marketing, administrative services, finance, and human resources.

The first step in this project was a series of meetings between the evaluators and the top-level managers from all major divisions of the corporation to clarify the purposes of the study and to identify what information would be useful to each of them. Next, the evaluators produced a design and plan for the evaluation and reviewed this document with the corporate leadership.

A manager within the human resources division of the company was given the responsibility for assisting the evaluators in actuating the project. He facilitated communications, convened the various committees, arranged interviews, helped distribute questionnaires, informed top management about the progress of the study, and provided critical planning and implementation advice to the evaluators. This internal liaison and project advocate was essential to the effectiveness of the study.

Two project advisory committees were formed of key managers. One committee, the steering committee, was made up of divisional leaders who had responsibility for the training and development of their employees. Another committee, the reference committee, was made up of all of the training managers from every division of the corporation. With approval from senior management for the basic evaluation design and general plan, the evaluators presented the design and plan to these two committees. Advisory group participants were asked what they wanted to learn from the study, how they hoped the study would affect the corporation, what problems they foresaw in the implementation of the evaluation, and how they wanted the findings reported to their group.

Steering committee members were asked to review data collection instruments (questionnaires and interview schedules) and procedures. Their input was very important to the quality of the data collection. Including them in this step kept them involved and maintained their sense of ownership in the evaluation.

Evaluators achieved a high level of involvement and commitment from company managers through the reporting process. Rather than use the typical approach of waiting until all of the data are collected and analyzed before reporting findings, white papers were prepared on eight different topics as the relevant data became available. The steering committee and reference committee decided which topics were of greatest importance to the company, and then the evaluators prepared and presented papers on each topic in a logical sequence. The evaluators described the findings, the implications of those findings for the company, and some preliminary recommendations that followed directly from those findings. Then the evaluators facilitated a meeting with the steering and reference committees, during which committee members further interpreted the data and added recommendations. Each report was transformed from the evaluators' report to the committee into the committee's report to the corporation.

Finally, the evaluators helped design and facilitate a series of action-planning sessions with steering committee members. During these workshops lasting up to two days in duration, participants identified the what, who, how, when, and with what resources of each of the recommendations that were generated from the white paper discussions. These workshops produced a strategic plan for applying a corporate-wide training and development process to the task of helping the company achieve its business objectives.

At the beginning of this project participants attended meetings because of an invitation that came from the senior managers of the corporation. By the end of the project participants were attending because of a belief that they could contribute to the success of the corporation through the enhancement of training and development.

Summary

Managers in organizations tend to lack commitment to the education of employees. They do not value training and development because they do not view educational activities on a par with corporate investments that bring significant returns to the business. However, training and development of all employees is critical to the success of any business today, and managerial input into the process of training and development is essential to its effective implementation. Therefore, the attitude of managers toward training and development must be changed. One key way to do this is to involve managers in the evaluation of the organization's educational programs. By collaborating with evaluators, managers can provide essential input into the design, implementation, and use of evaluations. They develop ownership in the results of the evaluation and, therefore, in the results of the training. The collaboration between managers and trainers that occurs in the process will help the organization use the training and development function to achieve its business objectives.

References

Alkin, M. C., Daillak, R., and White, P. *Using Evaluations: Does Evaluation Make a Difference?* Beverly Hills, Calif.: Sage, 1979.
Bernhard, H. B., and Ingols, C. A. "Six Lessons for the Corporate Classroom." *Harvard Business Review*, September–October 1988, p. 41.
Carnevale, A. P., Gainer, L. J., and Meltzer, A. S. *Workplace Basics: The Skills Employers Want.* Washington, D.C.: American Society for Training and Development and U.S. Department of Labor, 1989, p. 7.
Kirkpatrick, D. L. *Evaluating Training Programs.* Madison, Wisc.: American Society for Training and Development, 1975, pp. 1–17.
Patton, M. Q. *Utilization-Focused Evaluation.* Beverly Hills, Calif.: Sage, 1978.

Stephen Joel Gill is a principal in FERA (Formative Evaluation Research Associates, Inc.), an evaluation consulting firm located in Ann Arbor, Michigan. He is also director of human resources of FERA. He holds a Ph.D. in counseling psychology from Northwestern University and was professor in the School of Education at the University of Michigan from 1977 to 1984.

Analyzing evaluation services in a business training environment serves as a vehicle for deriving internal evaluation strategy.

Strategy for Internal Evaluators

Alan C. Nowakowski

My perception is that the evaluation literature is dominated by external evaluation issues and frameworks. Much of it is based on external evaluation work that is broad in scope, serving multiple audiences who often have conflicting values and information needs. Such external evaluation studies often attempt to evaluate all aspects of a program or project, including needs, goals, structure, and outcomes, as well as to negotiate relevant standards for doing so. It is challenging and important work. However, my experience has been that the issues and problems encountered in this type of evaluation do not transfer well to the issues that internal evaluators must resolve to provide effective evaluation service and products.

This chapter presents information about evaluation services provided in the Professional Education Division (PED) to support training at Arthur Andersen and Company. Following a high-level overview of evaluation services, detailed information is provided about a single service area—course development evaluation, which is internally referred to as pilot evaluation. Course development evaluation is highlighted because it provides a key to understanding factors that are important to building an effective internal evaluation capability. The way in which evaluation services evolved at PED is described. Characteristics of PED's internal evaluation services are contrasted with evaluation characteristics portrayed in the literature. Summary strategy suggestions are made that could prove useful to internal evaluators in other settings.

Organizational Context

Arthur Andersen and Company is a worldwide professional services organization with an extensive practice in accounting and audit and in tax, management information, and educational consulting. Statistics from the 1988 annual report indicate that the company has about forty-six thousand employees in 215 cities and 50 countries around the world. Total fees in 1988 were about $2.8 billion.

Arthur Andersen and Company has earned a reputation as a leader in professional education. A heavy commitment to training is part of its history and culture. It invests approximately 8 percent of firm revenues in training each year. Training is perceived not only as a vehicle for building necessary job skills but also as a means for transmitting firm culture. Internally, training has been referred to as "the glue that holds the firm together."

The firm's Center for Professional Education is located in St. Charles, Illinois, in what was originally a private liberal arts college. There are housing and classroom accommodations for about seventeen hundred people. About six hundred employees work at the Center. The Center's mission is to meet the internal training needs of the company's personnel. The firm provides training consulting services to clients, but client-related training services are provided through firm offices and not through the Center.

A team approach is used to develop the company's training programs. A project team is formed for each training-development effort. Each team is composed of office personnel who have the needed content knowledge and of education specialists from the Center who have expertise in training design and development. Major products produced for instructor-led training are an instructor guide and participant materials. Typically, the instructor guide is well documented so that a large number of office personnel with specified job experience and skills can later be used to teach the course. A permanent cadre of instructors is not used to teach courses at the Center, except in management development. Instead, an instructional team is formed of office line personnel each time a course is conducted. Office personnel are involved in training as participants and instructors throughout their careers with the firm. Although almost all of the company's internal training programs are developed through the Center, not all of them are centrally delivered. About 30 percent of the training is delivered at the Center; the rest is either self-study or instructor-led training that is done in the offices.

PED has a total active curriculum of about 850 courses or fourteen thousand training hours. The longest course in the curriculum is a three-week Management Information Consulting Division (MICD) course, which is preceded by a twelve-day self-study course. Mainline-type courses in any of the major practice divisions average about five days in length and are preceded by self-study courses. Many training programs in the curriculum are one to three days in length.

Evaluation Services Overview

An Evaluation Services Unit (ESU) has existed within PED for about ten years. Currently it is part of a larger organizational unit referred to as Research and Evaluation. ESU provides evaluation services to all educational program areas that have training-development responsibilities. Educational program areas within PED coincide with major practice areas, for example, tax, audit, and management information consulting. No organizational mandate exists to use ESU services. Requests for services are discretionary decisions of the educational program areas and project teams. However, some ESU services are so well established and have proved so beneficial that few development teams neglect using ESU services.

In general, all work in ESU revolves around two key training issues: *effectiveness* and *validity*. Effectiveness pertains to questions about the extent to which training outcomes match training goals: Was the training effective in accomplishing what it set out to do? Validity pertains to questions about the correctness or appropriateness of training goals: Are the training goals correct in relation to documented business problems? Do we have the right training? One or the other of these issues is at the core of all ESU service lines.

The two primary service lines provided by ESU are training needs assessment and training evaluation. The purpose of a needs assessment is to provide data to set valid training objectives. Validity is the central issue in a needs assessment. The primary purpose of training evaluation is to provide data for assessing the extent to which training objectives and needs are met. Effectiveness is the central issue in training evaluation.

Training evaluation subsequently can be focused at four commonly accepted assessment levels: *Level 1* is reaction—What do participants think about the training, what are their assessments? *Level 2* is learning—Have participants acquired the knowledge and skills taught? *Level 3* is performance—What impact has the training had on job performance? *Level 4* is organizational impact—What impact has the training had on organization indicators such as productivity, profitability, and turnover? The higher the level of assessment, the more complex and difficult evaluation becomes. Discussion of these different levels of training evaluation have proved useful in negotiating with decision makers about the types of effectiveness data they need, the usefulness of the data at each level, the costs and constraints involved in obtaining the data, and the risks of not obtaining them.

The training evaluation services provided by the ESU are needs assessment, course development evaluation, tests and measurement, and follow-up evaluation. *Needs assessment* refers to studies designed to ensure that training is targeted for the right people at the right time in their careers. *Course development evaluation* is a step in the training-development process and is a test of training materials before they are finalized for release to the field for ongoing delivery. *Tests and measurement* refers to technical assistance in the development and administration of educational tests and inventories to measure learning and learner characteristics. *Follow-up evaluation* refers to studies that examine the impact of training on job performance and the organization.

Needs assessments are performed at both the general curriculum and the more specific course levels. No single approach is followed. A broad range of data sources and techniques are used, including meetings, discussions, small-group processes, surveys, interviews, performance data reviews, and reanalysis of existing data bases. Study scope and procedures vary significantly by study. ESU is involved in about ten to fifteen needs assessment projects a year.

The tests and measurement service line provides assistance to educational program areas in developing reliable and valid instruments for measuring learning and learner characteristics. Test development is a joint effort with an educational program area. The development team is responsible for item writing. ESU's role is to assist in planning the test, formatting it, editing test items, processing test data, and performing reliability and validity studies. So far tests have been used primarily for assessing learning of self-study materials that are prerequisite to centralized schools and for waivers to test out of self-study materials.

Follow-up evaluations are a relatively new ESU service line. The primary problem has been to find cost-effective ways of evaluating training. It is not the case that PED's evaluation specialists do not know how to collect convincing impact data. Rather, the problem is that building the data base is often expensive. Additionally, in this environment many of the schools have evolved over time. Although there is no question about their overall effectiveness, the construction of a data base that provides hard evidence of this effectiveness is costly. Such data may be nice to have, but it does not make the training any better. Since evaluation resources are scarce, the working philosophy is generally that training development benefits more from up-front evaluation investment for needs assessment than it does for impact studies that reaffirm effectiveness and lead to fine tuning.

In a few cases follow-up studies have produced good value for the firm. For example, an initial success in follow-up evaluation was a study of the impact of Arthur Andersen and Company's introductory microcomputer course. ESU was requested to do a follow-up evaluation of the effectiveness of training personnel in two-day sessions on IBM personal computers. In focusing the study it became clear that management's interest was in learning whether personnel were using microcomputers in their work and not whether microcomputer skills had been acquired in the training school. Having identified management's primary interest, a survey study was conducted that provided reasonable estimates about current microcomputer use and, by including both trained and untrained personnel in the sample, also demonstrated a training effect. Although it was nice to be able to show a training effect, management's real interest was in applying the overall microcomputer use estimates as a basis for judging how well its total strategy, of which training was but a part, was working toward achieving integration of microcomputers into practice areas. The survey information proved useful, and ESU was requested to conduct the survey twice more at intervals of eighteen to twenty-four months in order to provide similar status estimates of the extent to which microcomputers were being integrated into practice areas.

Since the original microcomputer study, other follow-up evaluation studies have been successfully completed. Factors they share in common with the microcomputer studies are that they provided data on performance variables that were trackable and indicative of important changes that the firm was trying to institute. Training was but one of the multiple strategies used by management for achieving change. Separating training effects from other effects was not of primary concern to management. Not having to separate training effects from other variables typically results in simple designs that are cost effective. Management is provided with valuable information for determining whether an overall strategy is working or whether adjustments to strategy are needed.

Course Development Evaluation

Course development evaluation, or pilot evaluation, was the original service that led to the establishment of an evaluation unit within PED. It continues to be a principal area of the ESU's work. It exemplifies what works best in a business training environment and provides a vehicle for identifying factors that are important to effective internal evaluation.

Course development evaluation is a pilot test of draft training materials with a sample of the target training audience. It provides (1) a good indication of how a target population will react to a given piece of training before that training is released for general distribution; (2) a balanced perspective that is based on objective information used to gauge the effectiveness of individual instructional components and the training as a whole; and (3) a focus for the final steps in the training-development process by identifying particular instructional components that require revision.

The methodology for pilot evaluation consists of four work segments: planning and preliminary design, detailed design, implementation, and reporting. Each of those segments produces a different product. Planning and preliminary design produces a memo that documents the agreed-upon plan for the evaluation. Instruments and procedures are the products of detailed design. Raw data are the product of implementation, and a report is the product of the final phase, reporting.

Multiple data-gathering techniques are combined in various ways in performing course development evaluations. The typical pilot evaluation includes the following elements:

1. *Participant questionnaires.* The questionnaires are designed by the evaluator assigned to do the course development evaluation. They are put together based on a review of school materials and discussions with the development team regarding their informational needs and priorities. Questionnaires are designed to collect reactions at the end of modules, school days, and the school overall. Most of the items on the questionnaires are selected from a historical item pool. Typically, a few new items always are needed to address unique aspects or concerns of the school. Also, there is a set of seventeen standard items that are used for all schools. The standard items reflect variables that have a demonstrated relationship to school effectiveness in PED's environment. Ratings on these items serve as common standards for assessing school effectiveness. Low ratings on any of the common items are cause for concern and a basis for revising material.

2. *Observation.* The pilot conduct is observed by the evaluator. Observations are made regarding the extent to which the materials are used as designed. Changes to content and procedures are noted, and the amount of time spent on each agenda item is recorded for comparison to planned time estimates.

3. *Participant interviews.* The evaluator interviews participants about their reactions to training during breaks, meals, and sometimes at the end of a training day. Frequently, group debriefings are held by the evaluator following an important module, at the end of a training day, or at the end of the school.

4. *Instructor interviews.* Most instructor-led schools are team taught with an instructor-to-participant ratio of about one to twelve. The evaluator interviews all instructors who participate in the pilot.

Pilot evaluation results are processed daily. Participants record their answers to closed-ended items on machine-scoreable answer sheets. Questionnaires are collected daily, scanned, and computer processed so that the instructors and design team receive computer printouts of questionnaire data each morning from the preceding school day. At the end of the school, the evaluator meets with the development team to give them a preliminary debriefing of evaluation findings. This debriefing provides the development team with basic data for outlining a revision work plan and time schedule. The final evaluation report is provided to the development team within ten working days of the end of the school.

The course development evaluation report averages about ten pages in length. The following is an outline of a typical pilot evaluation report:
- *Section 1*. Evaluation purpose, data gathering techniques and a list of attachments
- *Section 2*. Description of school participants and comparison to target audience
- *Section 3*. Quality rating of each module and school overall
- *Section 4*. Features, issues, and qualifiers
- *Section 5*. School strengths
- *Section 6*. Points for consideration.

The course development evaluation is a very streamlined report. Each is composed of six basic sections plus attachments, the latter providing lower levels of detail and supporting data and documentation for the high-level findings contained in the overall report. Section 5 of the outline, identification of strengths, is especially important in this type of evaluation since, in the revision process, steps are taken to protect those aspects of the school that are functioning effectively. Per Section 6, data sources and statistics that document the degree to which a problem exists are referenced to support each improvement point suggested. In report attachments, all conclusions about school strengths and weaknesses, from major high-level points to minor module-specific points, are listed in column format with cross-references to data sources, data gathering techniques, and summary data.

There are three summary points about course development evaluation that need to be emphasized:

1. Course development evaluation methodology has been documented in detail. Each segment has been broken into tasks, the purpose of each tasks explained, and the steps for performing each task outlined. Moreover, besides indicating what is to be done, exemplary products are provided for each step in the process. This type of documentation provides new evaluation personnel with clear direction for doing the work. It helps ensure quality work and minimizes the amount of supervision needed to obtain quality work. Although it may sound mechanical, in practice the methodology is flexible, so that the comprehensiveness of the evaluation is related to the degree of risk and the importance of the training being evaluated, and so that individuals assigned the work have the opportunity to exercise their creativity in combining, experimenting

with and refining techniques to enhance and leave their mark on the methodology.

2. The purpose of course development evaluation is to judge audience acceptance of the prereleased training and to assess the relative effectiveness of instructional components. Relevant criteria for making these assessments have evolved over time. Standard questions and scales have been developed to gather data on these criteria. Such data are being collected on about fifty to sixty-five course development evaluations per year. As this data base grows, its usefulness increases in relation to a broad range of evaluation and research questions, including further clarification and refinement criteria for evaluating training products prior to release for ongoing delivery.

3. The data-gathering techniques used in course development evaluations are not sophisticated and certainly not new or even innovative. Any of the data-gathering techniques on which ESU relies, if used alone, would likely produce weak, flawed, and poor evaluations. However, evaluative power is obtained by combining these relatively straightforward techniques. For example, an experienced observer armed with participant questionnaires and interviews, group debriefings, and instructor reactions has multiple measures from multiple data sources to formulate and substantiate conclusions. Gathering comparable data on relevant standards or criterion scales across instructional components within a training school provides clear direction with minimal risk of making wrong decisions about where to focus revision efforts in order to produce the best payoff.

Factors Contributing to Effective Internal Evaluation

Course development evaluation is perceived as effective and useful evaluation at Arthur Andersen and Company. There are four factors that appear to be important to an understanding of this success. These factors are quality evaluation product, defined evaluation methodology, cost efficiency, and service orientation. The *quality evaluation product* is evaluation information that (1) supports decision making and action planning; (2) is credible or believable to information users so that barriers to assimilating the information are minimized; (3) is technically sound information so that risks in applying the information are minimized; and (4) is timely so that the information is available when needed.

Many of the characteristics important to *defined evaluation methodology* were identified in the preceding section. Essentially, the methodology requires that (1) product specifications are clear with exemplary work products provided; (2) procedures for doing the work are documented; (3) standards or criterion scales for evaluating or reporting quality are clearly defined; and (4) roles and responsibilities of those involved in the evaluation are specified and documented.

Primary considerations regarding *cost efficiency* are productivity and benefit. Productivity refers to how much it costs to produce the evaluation product. As noted throughout this chapter, good methodology is important to achieving high productivity. Methodology provides a way to obtain efficiency and ensure product quality. Other critical factors are the skills and experience of evaluation personnel. Benefit refers to the value or organizational gain obtained from resources used to produce the evaluation product. In PED's environment, the variables for assessing the evaluation's contribution or benefit involve the extent to which evaluation recommendations are implemented and the impact they have on the quality and effectiveness of PED training products.

Service orientation is a mode of operation, or a general perspective, that guides the evaluation. It means that evaluation personnel place a high value on producing a useful product in a way that is sensitive to the requirements and constraints of the situation. Important characteristics include (1) flexibility in applying methodology to the situation; (2) responsiveness in adapting to user time frames, schedules, and resources; (3) innovativeness with appropriate risk taking to meet changing needs and requirements; and (4) balancing service and integrity to meet the goal of responsiveness. To a great extent the operational definition of this mode is simply hard work geared to meet user needs and requirements.

These four factors essentially tell us that successful internal evaluation is dependent on the production of a quality evaluation that contributes to the well-being of the organization, both in a consistent way and at a reasonable cost.

Evolution of Evaluation Services

ESU services are not all at the same stage of development. Major evaluation service lines have evolved in the following order: course development evaluation, needs assessment, testing, and follow-up evaluation. Course development evaluation, the starting point, focused primarily on training-effectiveness issues at a participant and instructor-reactions level. Successful course development service created a climate of trust that enabled the evaluators to raise sensitive validity questions during the needs assessment. Needs assessment was followed by evaluation of training effectiveness at a deeper level than participant reactions. Learning objectives were measured through testing. Follow-up evaluation, which focuses on the tough questions about transfer of learning to job performance and organizational impact, was the last piece to fall in place.

Each evaluation service line addresses a perceived need of the training organization. Each has achieved a level of success on all four factors sufficient to justify its continued development.

Contrasts with Evaluation Literature

As indicated earlier, I believe that the evaluation literature is dominated by external evaluation issues and frameworks that differ significantly from the problems that internal evaluators, particularly in the private sector, typically encounter. Significant differences exist in the areas of evaluation scope, audience, standards, and the emphasis or importance of evaluator independence.

In the evaluation literature the frameworks and cases reported are often broad and comprehensive in scope. Much effort is devoted to understanding the evaluation context. Often all aspects of the evaluation object are under examination, including goals and objectives, inputs, process and procedures, and products and outcomes. In contrast, internal evaluation functions such as those performed at PED are much narrower in scope, focusing on a particular aspect of a project at a point in its life cycle.

A second area of difference pertains to evaluation audience. Much attention is given in the literature to the need to serve multiple audiences. The audiences, or stakeholders, as they are often referred to, are diverse in terms of competing needs and values. This diversity significantly influences how the evaluation is designed, conducted, reported, and used, as well as the role of the evaluator and how the evaluator is perceived. Compared to the private sector, such complications would seem to be more of a problem in the public sector, where accountability for decisions is less clear, and more of a problem for external evaluators, where scope is broad, than for internal evaluators with their tightly focused evaluations, particularly those internal evaluators operating in the private sector. At PED evaluation use is closely tied to decision making and accountability. The organization defines accountability for a decision in a reasonably clear way. Thus for internal evaluation studies at PED, there is typically a single primary audience or decision maker for the evaluation findings, not multiple audiences of comparable importance that need to be served. When lines of accountability are clear, the decision maker, as opposed to the evaluator, is held responsible for resolving value conflicts that may exist, which simplifies the role of the evaluator and the evaluation process.

A third area of difference is that of standards for making value judgments about the object of evaluation. The standard applied in internal evaluations is in general better defined and understood than that applied in external evaluations. The reasons are that external evaluations typically cover a broader area than internal evaluations, so that there are more standards to define and apply, and external evaluators in general have both less time and less knowledge of the organization for defining standards. Internal evaluators not only have more knowledge about the organization for defining value standards but, more important, also have the opportunity to incrementally refine and validate standards over time. I believe that defining and refining standards for evaluation of an object is the area in which internal evaluators can make their most significant contribution to the organization.

A fourth area of difference is that of evaluator independence. Evaluator independence has a pervasive effect on evaluation methods, procedures, and results. The importance placed on independence with respect to external evaluation is understandable. Often an important reason for obtaining an external evaluation is to obtain an outside perspective. An independent perspective has inherent value, and it is important to have at times. However, the principle of evaluator independence does not have the same importance to the internal evaluator as it does to the external evaluator. The parallel concept or principle of comparable worth to the internal evaluator is that of collaboration. The internal evaluator contributes most from a position of collaboration, being a team member and applying evaluation skills and expertise to help the team achieve its objectives.

Evaluation Strategy Suggestions

Based on analysis of the internal evaluation services of PED, the following summary points are given as evaluation strategy suggestions for internal evaluators.

Concentrate on Effectiveness Issues. Begin by helping the organization achieve its goals. Put evaluation to work to maximize return on committed resources. At any point in time, most organizational resources are committed to specified goals. Having made these commitments, organizational attention is focused rightly on meeting these goals to obtain expected returns. Internal evaluation resources should be similarly focused. The majority of evaluation resources should be allocated to obtaining and providing data to help maximize goal attainment. Effectiveness data can be obtained at different assessment levels and performance checkpoints, so that even with limited resources one should be able to produce useful evaluative feedback. The best way to help the organization with validity issues is by finding acceptable ways to assist with goal-setting activities that occur on the front end of projects and programs.

Provide Evaluation to Service Management Quality Control Points. There are performance points where scheduled management reviews are conducted. Major checkpoints at PED include review of training goals, training design, and development test tryouts. The purpose of these reviews is to obtain management commitment and direction for moving forward. Since these reviews are recognized decision points, if systematic data about performance are available, they are likely to be used and to benefit multiple groups, that is, those doing the review and those affected by its results. If performance results are as expected, the process moves forward as planned; if there are problems, the data provide a basis for solving them.

Service Areas with High-Volume Potential. Efficiency requires learning and repeated experience. No one is highly efficient on the first try. If each evaluation study is a new and different experience, it may be interesting and challenging, but is not likely to be highly efficient. Repeated similar experiences are necessary to build proficiency and efficiency. The documentation of evaluation procedures in methodology provides the basis for training and leveraging the evaluation work to entry-level evaluation personnel, which results in further efficiency gains.

Establish Performance Indicators for Key Success Factors. Key success factors are those few procedures that must go well to ensure success. They represent managerial areas that should be given special and continued attention to bring about high performance. Four key success factors that are important to providing effective internal evaluation at PED are quality evaluation product, defined evaluation methodology, cost efficiency, and service orientation. Earlier, each factor was defined in terms of a number of characteristics or performance dimensions. Establishing performance indicators for these dimensions and gathering data to determine the extent to which expectations are met can provide internal evaluators with a useful framework for managing and developing an effective evaluation capability. When defining performance indicators, make them action oriented; for example, final written evaluation reports on course development are due within ten days of school completion. Performance expectations with respect to individual evaluation service lines should be raised as the service line evolves from early development to maturity.

Manage Growth and Development. The provision of effective evaluation service requires developmental resources. It takes time, effort, and repeated experience to develop proficiency and supporting methodology for evaluation practice. Do not spread resources too thin by developing too many evaluation service lines simultaneously. Doing so usually reduces the probability of success and increases the cost of achieving it. Also, from a staff development viewpoint, it is preferable to have evaluation services lines at different stages in their life cycle. In this fashion, skills required to perform the work will vary and staff can be leveraged effectively. More experienced personnel can be used to do more complicated work in areas where methodology is less defined. Less experienced personnel can do work in areas where the methodology is better defined. A broad range of work is created that is challenging to personnel at different levels, and individual personnel are provided with opportunities for growth and development, which together result in enhanced efficiency and effectiveness of the evaluation unit as a whole.

Focus on Defining and Refining Evaluation Standards. Standards for assessing merit and worth are critical to effective evaluation. Standard setting is also highly problematical. This is apparent in the literature, especially in evaluation studies of broad scope, where ambiguous accountability for decisions and conflicting values among stakeholders prevail. Internal evaluators have a major advantage regarding standard setting. Internal evaluators have a greater opportunity than external evaluators to learn decision-maker and organizational values and to accumulate data across time and projects in order to refine and validate standards. Better-defined standards lead to more effective evaluation efforts.

Use Collaboration as an Underlying Principle. See yourself as a member of the team. Recognize that as an internal evaluator your primary value is in the application of specialized skills and expertise, as opposed to the provision of an independent view of the team and its effort. By functioning as a trusted member of the team, an internal evaluator has access to more data, resulting in a better basis for problem analysis and recommendations to help the team achieve its objectives.

Alan C. Nowakowski is a training director in the Professional Education Division (PED) at Arthur Andersen and Company. He has worked in research and development at PED and formerly was a director of evaluation for a school district and a staff member in a university evaluation center.

A discussion of some obstacles that an evaluator of training confronts and of promising directions for more successful practice.

Evaluation of Training by Trainers

Nicholas M. Sanders

Although some businesses now have dedicated program evaluation positions in their training-development and delivery process, and some may even call in external professional evaluators for large-scale reviews of their training efforts (see Jerrell, 1984), a large portion of the training in business settings is evaluated by persons with very little or no formal education in program evaluation. Evaluation of training is often conducted by trainers themselves (who have, on the average, less education about and experience with program evaluation than school teachers) and by clients of the trainers, for example, target audience managers or company executives (who have even less background experience with evaluation of training programs).

In this article, I present some salient characteristics of the actual evaluation practices of trainers, in contrast to the practices suggested by the professional training literature on evaluation. I then discuss my observations about the factors involved in this contrast between approaches.

The author greatly appreciates the opportunity provided by his employer, CIGNA Corporation, to write this chapter. However, the views expressed in the chapter are those of the author and should not be construed as the position of CIGNA or of any other CIGNA employee.

Finally, I identify several forces within the training profession and the broader business environment that evaluators might attend to in order to construct productive evaluations of training.

Evaluation Practices Within the Training Profession

From my experiences as an insurance and computer systems trainer who has developed systematic evaluation training for fellow trainers, I have found that trainers' and their clients' definitions of the term *evaluation* are closer to the ordinary language meaning of the term than they are to the definitions used in the evaluation profession: evaluation of a training program implies that one gathers qualified others' evaluations of the program. Usually the qualified others are (1) the experts who know the topic of training and the job setting to which the training applies and (2) the trainees who have experienced the training. Thus, these evaluations of training usually consist of reviews of the program by subject-matter experts and completion of evaluation forms by trainees. The reviews by the experts are the basis of the formative evaluation, while the trainees' evaluations, completed immediately after the training event, serve as the summative evaluation.

Formative Evaluation in the Training Literature. In the training literature the notion of evaluation is not limited to the above meanings. Major discussions of instructional design for the training profession include sections on formative evaluation that focus on tryouts of training materials with at least one trainee from the target audience (see, for example, Blank, 1982, pp. 251-260).

Also, recent considerations of evaluation of training have presented formative evaluation as including many techniques other than reviews by subject-matter experts. Most prominent are tryouts with small samples of trainees from the target population (Arnoff, 1987; Brandenburg and Smith, 1986). Brandenburg and Smith (1986, p. 14) list the following as the common, formative course evaluation techniques mentioned in the training literature: content analysis by subject-matter experts, participant reaction questionnaires, in-class achievement tests, classroom observation, participant interviews and debriefings, videotape of classroom and participants, and instructor opinions or interviews. Thus, although the most common technique used in training evaluations, expert review is only one the several techniques promoted and reported in the training literature.

Summative Evaluation in the Training Literature. The training literature is also broad with regard to the focus of summative evaluations. Trade publication articles on evaluations frequently cite Kirkpatrick's (1987) presentations of evaluation concepts for trainers. Kirkpatrick (p. 302) cautions that although at present business management rarely

expects training to yield good returns, such as they would expect from the sales and manufacturing departments, they may begin to have such expectations about training. To be prepared, he alerts trainers to four foci of training-program evaluation. Because he sees the foci as building on one another, he calls them "logical steps," as follows:
- *Step 1: Reaction.* How well did the conferees like the program?
- *Step 2: Learning.* What principles, facts, and techniques were learned? What attitudes were changed?
- *Step 3: Behavior.* What changes in job behavior resulted from the program?
- *Step 4: Results.* What were the tangible results of the program in terms of reduced cost, improved quality, improved quantity, and so on?

The previously mentioned evaluation form, administered to trainees to gather their evaluations immediately after the training event, corresponds to Kirkpatrick's Step 1. However, the other steps, or foci, are not usually considered. In view of the income-generating and cost-reduction (that is, "bottom line") orientation that businesses are reputed to have, it is a surprise that the trainee evaluation form is considerable more popular in the evaluation of training than indicators of improved job performance.

The relative popularity of the reaction form in evaluation of training is also in contrast with its status in evaluation in other areas. Think for a moment that the reactions of students in school programs, if obtained at all and unless very negative, do not generally play much of a role in the overall evaluation of the programs.

At this point, the story comes to mind of the CEO of a large corporation that was in the midrange of financial outcomes when compared to its competitors. This CEO received a high percentage of "superior" self-ratings from members of his management team. He did not sign off on any of them but instead returned them. He asked his managers how they could be "superior" when their corporation was only average. Similarly, trainees' superior ratings of training can easily occur without superior learning and transfer to the work setting. Evaluation of training would definitely be strengthened by increased attention to the other aspects of evaluation promoted by Kirkpatrick.

Methodological Problems. In addition to limiting themselves to trainees' evaluation reactions, trainers may not obtain valid reaction results. While trainers are alert to problems of the phrasing of evaluation form items (such as loaded questions), their lack of education in research methods leaves them relatively blind to some methodological problems. Although one should definitely not expect an understanding of research design details, some elementary methodological principles are not followed.

In particular, there are problems with aspects of evaluation form administration, collection, and analysis with which trainers are usually not familiar. One of these is the concern for obtaining reactions from all of a small or locally concentrated group of trainees or of a representative sample from a large, diverse group. In addition, there is at times a lack of concern for administration of evaluation forms, so that some trainees influence the reports of others (when forms are completed in group or workstation settings).

Another methodological difficulty that I frequently encounter is the lack of systematic consideration of differences in outcomes among different groups of trainees; trainers do not routinely compare evaluations by trainees at different levels of experience or with different job responsibilities. At times, too, there should be a concern for important group differences and for the appropriate unit of analysis, as when trainees in different field locations do not respond to the training in the same way. In such cases, when the individual trainee is the unit of analysis and ratings are combined across locations, the results will of course lead to inappropriate conclusions, and a potentially important finding of group differences will be ignored.

Factors Affecting the Evaluation Practices of Trainers

The trainers' reliance on trainees' reactions for summative evaluations of their training and their disregard for the methodological problems mentioned above seem to be the result of a number of factors. Some of these factors support the use of trainee reactions; others operate against consideration of the other foci of evaluation.

What Supports the Predominant Use of Trainee Evaluation Reactions? First, as presented earlier in this chapter, the use of evaluations from qualified others, such as trainees who know the details of the training program, fits the ordinary or everyday notion of evaluation more than any other source of definition.

The trainees' evaluation forms are also popular as bases for reports to clients, who have a management or a management support staff relation to the trainees. These clients are very interested in the reactions of the trainees, for whom they have arranged the training. Clients want to know whether these people are saying good things or bad things about the training; the reactions to the training will reflect on the client as well as the trainer.

In addition, because training is available within a company as a support service, its existence depends on the involvement of the trainee population. Trainees are potential participants in future training programs, as are their managers and co-workers to whom they are likely to comment about the training. It makes good sense for the trainer to determine what the trainees are likely to say about the program and what they think might be done to improve it.

Finally, solicitation of a trainee's reaction to the training is in itself a communication of respect for the viewpoint of the trainee. For this reason, it may be considered by the trainee as an added positive feature of the training program. In situations where the trainee is of equal or higher status in comparison with the trainer, such solicitation of reaction can also serve to acknowledge the atypical status of the trainee, since trainees are usually in a subordinate role to the trainer.

What Operates Against the Use of Other Evaluation Information Sources? By contrast, Kirkpatrick's other foci of (or "steps" in) training-program evaluation—learning, behavior, and results—pose difficulties for trainers. One difficulty arises from testing trainees to determine achievement of the training program's objectives; testing is associated with the impractical information and the demeaning status experienced during childhood in school. Having a strong need to be solicitous to trainees, the average trainer is resistant to testing adult and sometimes high-status trainees.

This resistance to testing has formal support in the literature on "adult learning," a subject domain that deals with the need to change the predominantly autocratic teacher-student relationship that essentially everyone is exposed to as a child, in order to help adults learn more effectively and efficiently. Malcolm Knowles, one of the best-known thinkers in the domain of adult learning (or "andragogy," as he calls it), has this to say about evaluation (Knowles, 1987, p. 176):

> In many situations institutional policies require some sort of "objective" (quantitative) measure of learning outcomes (Kirkpatrick, Scriven, Stufflebeam). But the recent trend in evaluation research has been to place increasing emphasis on "subjective" (qualitative) evaluation—finding out what is really happening inside the participants and how differently they are performing in life (Cronbach, Guba and Lincoln, Patton). In any case, the andragogical model requires that the learners be actively involved in the process of evaluating their learning outcomes.

The use of testing for achievement of a training program's objectives would be identified as an "objective (quantitative) measure of learning outcomes" and as a process of evaluating that does not actively involve trainees; the andragogical model has an antitest orientation.

More generally, the andragogical model implies a lack of standardized procedure for gathering information. When the trainer involves each group of trainees in the determination of what evaluation will be conducted for their particular group, not only might the evaluation differ from occasion to occasion, but it also might not reveal information important to a sufficient evaluation. For example, in an interpersonal skills-training program for managers, one group of trainees might choose to focus the evaluation on skills of persuasion and another group might take sympathetic listening skills as its focus—while neither includes evaluation of the major program objective of knowing the situational contingencies that determine which skill should be utilized.

Other factors operating against the learning, behavior, and results foci of evaluation are revealed in a recent survey of twelve hundred American Society for Training and Development (ASTD) members by Grider, Capps, and Toombs (1988). These researchers found that while the trainee reaction type of evaluation was used more often than the behavior, results, and learning foci (even by this professionally oriented ASTD membership), ASTD members considered other foci of evaluation to be more effective. Why do these trainers settle for the reaction-type form and not use other, more job-performance-oriented foci that they consider more effective? The respondents in the survey gave several reasons: the more job-performance-oriented foci were considered too time consuming, too expensive, and beyond their level of expertise. By comparison, the evaluation forms completed by trainees are easy to construct, cheap to produce, and quick to administer and analyze.

Issues of available time and funds are, of course, issues of resource allocation by a business's management. If obtaining information about increased learning, transfer to the job, and impact on business results was considered sufficiently important, then the necessary adjustments would be made in job requirements and budget. In addition, consultation and professional development would be encouraged in order to build the needed evaluation expertise of the trainees.

At present, however, a very influential force in time and funds allocation for many businesses is *productivity*. Productivity refers to the number of products completed within a given unit of time (or the time required to bring a given product to completion). While this concept is most easily applied in manufacturing, it has also been used in other types of work, including provision of services. However, a production orientation—with an extreme emphasis on quantity—can have an adverse effect on product quality and on the provision of more than perfunctory service.

In training, a production orientation is manifest in concerns for counts of training products developed (having a large number of products "on the shelf") and of persons exposed to training events (for example, number attending workshops). In such an environment a trainer who is busy developing the next product or offering another workshop is unlikely to spend time collecting information on transfer of training to the jobs of previous trainees, some of whom may even be working in different locations around the world. Even if conducted, this type of follow-up could be seen as a delay in completing the project and, therefore, as a decrease in productivity.

Factors Affecting Formative Evaluation Practices. A production orientation adversely affects formative evaluation as well. While the reviews carried out by subject-matter experts are considered necessary to certify the accuracy and completeness of training content under development, other techniques for formative evaluation are not normally used. Omitted, in particular, are tryouts with small samples from the target population to determine trainee reactions and learning during the training-development process. Such tryouts obviously would require time to prepare and conduct, resulting in a delay in the completion of the training product. Tryouts also entail drawing the trainees from their work, thereby decreasing their productivity. Generally, the lack of tryouts for formative evaluation is supported by the belief that a good trainer will be able to anticipate tryout results and will build those anticipations into the training.

As a result of the reluctance to conduct tryouts of training prior to official delivery, the early deliveries of the training become tryouts. Evaluations of the early deliveries are used to determine need for revisions. In fact, at least one training professional (Pearlstein, 1988) has suggested ongoing formative evaluation of training products already being delivered, in order to accommodate changing target populations and changing organizational environments.

Although such delayed formative evaluation may seem to serve the same purpose as a tryout prior to official delivery, it is not as satisfactory. A structured-response evaluation form from which responses can be easily counted and averaged is much more likely to be used than techniques more often associated with formative evaluation—close observation and questioning of the trainee about the training as it progress. Because evaluation of official deliveries is conducted primarily to report to others, usually training management and clients, the information sought is general and, with the structured-response form for easy summary, not the kind that pinpoints areas of needed improvement.

Another reason that a tryout type of formative evaluation may not be considered necessary is related to the omission of learning, job behavior, and business results in the summative evaluation. When the summative evaluation is not oriented to what the trainee knows or is able to do as a result of the training, there is much less to study in a tryout, that is, there are no knowledge achievement or skill competencies to assess.

On the other hand, for trainees' evaluation reactions that are so popular in summative evaluations, it may be that tryouts with a sample of the trainee population are not sufficiently useful in guiding revisions to warrant the added cost and time required. Trainee evaluation reactions may be more the result of emotional aspects of the training, such as comfort level created, that are difficult to build into a training program and therefore do not lend themselves to improvement for individual programs.

Taken together, the factors mentioned above form an environment that is hostile to a complete and systematic evaluation of training programs. There are, however, potentially supportive orientations that are influential within the training profession and within the broader world of business management.

Supportive Orientations for Change

In the following discussion, I examine those orientations—"performance analysis" in the training profession and "quality management" in the broader business environment—that I believe have the potential to support a more complete, systematic evaluation of training by trainers.

Performance Analysis. Within the training profession there is an orientation that favors use of performance analysis in determining training needs and assessing training success. Rummler (1987, p. 242) presents this orientation in comparison with others and defines the process in this way: "*Performance analysis* is a relatively new (20 years) but proven process for determining training needs and improving individual and organization performance. . . . The essence of this approach is the determination of the performance context of the trainee, and therefore the training input is directly linked to individual and organization performance."

Based on Rummler's outline of performance analysis (p. 229), there are three major steps, as follows: (1) Determine how the work of each trainee group influences the performance of the business organization as a whole. Determine what are (or should be) the critical job accomplishments and how each is critical. (2) Determine what tasks are required to produce the critical accomplishments. And (3) determine what knowledge or skills are required to perform these critical tasks. Training then is designed to provide whatever knowledge or skills, identified in the third step, are lacking among the trainees. These steps contrast with a more standard training needs assessment, which involves asking members of the trainee population or of management for their opinions of what training is needed.

Because the standard training needs assessment does not necessarily focus on job behavior or linkage to the business organization's results, it does not encourage evaluation of training based on changes in those criteria. Perhaps one indication that an organization will not support evaluation of training that focuses on job behavior and business results is its use of the standard assessment procedure to determine its training needs.

The performance analysis approach, on the other hand, does directly identify specific changes in individual and organizational performances as the reasons for the training, an orientation that implies that these performances should be assessed in order to evaluate the training. Thus, with a performance analysis approach the climate for evaluation of training is likely to include study of the learning, behavior, and results sources of information, as described by Kirkpatrick (1987). To the extent that an organization supports a performance analysis approach to training needs assessment, the extra time, resources, and expertise required for the more extensive evaluation will be available. In addition, in such an organization one will likely find tryouts for formative evaluation prior to official delivery of the training because more revisions would likely be required to fine-tune the training in order to result in the particular needed performance change(s) identified by the performance analysis.

In sum, the aspects of evaluation by trainers that I have identified as usually missing would probably not be missing in organizations that support a performance analysis orientation to training. Of course, because performance analysis is more time consuming and requires greater expertise than the standard opinion-based training needs assessment, one is less likely to find organizations that support it.

Quality Management. There is, however, another force—one operating in the broader business environment—that can foster performance analysis (and, thereby, the related job behavior and business results evaluations conducted by trainers). That force is the "quality management process"(see, for example, Deming, 1981-1982).

Among the key features of the quality management process is the focus on the processes involved in developing and delivering a business's products or services. The emphasis is on avoiding defects by improving these processes, not by quality controlling the defective products or services after they are completed. A focus on process implies both (1) an identification of the specific component activities that lead to the completed product or service, indicating how each contributes, and (2) a way to measure and analyze the functioning of each of those component activities. These implications of the quality management process are functionally the same as the first step of performance analysis, in which there is a study of how specifically the work of each trainee group affects the performance of the business organization as a whole.

Another key feature of the quality management process is a concern for ongoing improvement of the process. A related central belief associated with quality management is that there is no end to the possibilities for improvement. This orientation requires ongoing monitoring of the production or service process, involving standardized and reliable measurement, sampling, and statistical analysis. One implication of this feature is that the results of the monitoring can be used in training evaluation as job behavior information with explicit connections to the business results of the organization. Furthermore, because the monitoring is continuous and not specifically related to the training event, it can be considered nonreactive and unobtrusive in relation to the training.

A third essential feature of the quality management process is its way of defining *quality*. Quality is determined through customer satisfaction, not by conformance to design specifications or judgment by an employee assigned to assure or control quality. An additional aspect of the quality definition is the definition of the *customer,* for any given department in a business, as anyone inside the business, as well as outside, who depends on the output of the part of the production or service process managed in that department.

For a training department, one can draw the implication, as May (1987) does, that its customers are the trainees inasmuch as the trainees are the one who most directly depend on the output of the training department. While this orientation would seem to imply a support of the trainee reaction evaluation forms as the principal source of information for an evaluation, there are two significant elaborations of this conclusion.

First, within a quality managed business, the employees are directly involved in the monitoring of their part of the production or service process, and therefore they are quite familiar with the critical aspects of their job and how their work fits into the larger process. This knowledge should expand their capability of evaluating how well a training program will contribute to their work, assuming those types of questions are included in the trainee reaction evaluation form they are asked to complete.

Second, within a quality management process, the customers of training programs would not only be the trainees but also the trainees' managers and the clients who directly arrange for the training. These customers would have a strong need for evaluation based on the training's effects on the production or service process. Thus, these customers would be looking for evaluation information beyond the trainees' reactions alone.

The additional time and expertise that this more elaborate evaluation requires may be accepted within a quality management context; proponents of quality management point out that the costs of avoiding defects in the first place are less than paying for both their production and their correction. In addition, the quality management orientation emphasizes that commitment to quality management must permeate the organization, starting with and requiring the continuous support of the senior management. With this level of support, an environment conducive to a complete and systematic evaluation of training would exist.

Summary

I have observed substantial discrepancies between the evaluation practices described in the literature oriented to trainers and the actual evaluation practices of trainers. The literature provides direction for evaluating a wide range of foci on which to base program evaluation. Trainers usually attend to only one of these, their trainees' reactions to the training, and omit investigation of acquisition of new knowledge and skills, positive transfer to work, and improved business results. The literature also includes in the training-development process tryouts with samples of the intended audience. Trainers usually rely, however, on what they can obtain from training-material reviews by subject-matter experts and from their own understanding of the target population.

In the preceding discussion, I have identified some factors that I believe cause these discrepancies: trainers' lack of formal education in evaluation foci and methods; trainers' and training clients' preoccupation with trainee satisfaction; trainers' statuses in relation to their trainees; trainers' and clients' distrust of testing and quantitative methods; and a production orientation in the trainers' business organization environments.

Anyone proposing to alter the evaluation practices of trainers certainly has more to do than merely teaching how evaluation should be done or designing a model evaluation of training. There is a complex of factors—a culture—that works against a complete, systematic evaluation. In a given organization, that culture must be analyzed and at times challenged.

There are, however, some potentially supportive orientations current in the training profession and in the world of business management. One of these orientations is a performance analysis orientation to training, which emphasizes the detailed relationship of the job performance of an individual employee to the performance of the business as a whole and directs training and the evaluation of training to those individual job performances of the trainees. The other potentially supportive orientation discussed is quality management, which also focuses on job performance and continuous monitoring of the production process that can serve as an information source in the evaluation of training. When evaluators operate in these environments, they may be able to use both the quality management and the performance analysis orientations to support complete and systematic evaluations of training.

References

Arnoff, S. "Evaluation Issues in the Education Product Life-Cycle." In L. S. May, C. A. Moore, and S. J. Zammit (eds.), *Evaluating Business and Industry Training*. Boston: Kluwer-Nijhoff, 1987.

Blank, W. E. *Handbook for Developing Competency-Based Training Programs.* Englewood Cliffs, N.J.: Prentice-Hall, 1982.

Brandenburg, D. C., and Smith, M. E. *Evaluation of Corporate Training Programs.* Report no. 91. Princeton, N.J.: ERIC Clearinghouse on Tests, Measurements, and Evaluation, 1986.

Deming, W. E. "Improvement of Quality and Productivity Through Action by Management." *National Productivity Review,* Winter 1981-82.

Grider, D. T., Capps, C. J., and Toombs, L. A. "Evaluating Evaluations." *Training and Development Journal,* 1988, *42* (11), 11-12.

Jerrell, J. M. (ed.). "Evaluation Experience in Business Settings." *Evaluation News,* 1984, *5* (4), 15-58.

Kirkpatrick, D. L. "Evaluation." In R. L. Craig (ed.), *Training and Development Handbook.* (3rd ed.) New York: McGraw-Hill, 1987.

Knowles, M. S. "Adult Learning." In R. L. Craig (ed.), *Training and Development Handbook.* (3rd ed.) New York: McGraw-Hill, 1987.

May, L. S. "Applying Quality Management Concepts and Techniques to Training Evaluation." In L. S. May, C. A. Moore, and S. J. Zammit (eds.), *Evaluating Business and Industry Training.* Boston: Kluwer-Nijhoff, 1987.

Pearlstein, G. "Gathering Formative Evaluation Data Daily." *Performance & Instruction,* 1989, *27* (10), 49-50.

Rummler, G. A. "Determining Needs." In R. L. Craig (ed.), *Training and Development Handbook.* (3rd ed.) New York: McGraw-Hill, 1987.

Nicholas M. Sanders, Ph.D., has taught cognitive processes, measurement, and research methods at The Pennsylvania State University and worked as an evaluator for Research for Better Schools in Philadelphia. He continues his evaluation work as an adjunct to his work as a trainer in business settings.

The business environment and culture dictate expectations for economic impact of training that must be understood by evaluators.

Everything Important in Business and Industry Is Evaluated

Richard A. Swanson

The mission and goal of business and industry are to maximize the economic return on investment through the production and sale of goods and services. The milieu in which this activity takes place is complex and fluid. The "business" of the private sector is no easy matter. The vulnerability of individual employees, departments, and the organization itself goes beyond the day-to-day experience of most people who work in and with the public sector.

It is in the private sector context of competitiveness and change that business decision makers must operate. In contrast, most program evaluation experts have a public sector orientation.

Recently, in my home state of Minnesota, Pillsbury Company was purchased by a British firm, and Control Data Corporation laid off thirty-five hundred workers in St. Paul. Northwest Airlines was threatened by a hostile takeover by a rich industrialist from out West. Concurrently, the Twin Cities of Minneapolis and St. Paul report a very healthy economy and a low unemployment rate. During the same time period, the University of Minnesota has not had a single takeover threat, nor has any other Minnesota public sector organization experienced one, though the donation-supported and nonprofit Minnesota Ballet recently went out of business. A year from now I am sure there will be similar reports about other Minnesota organizations, with the great bulk of the news being from the private sector.

Business decision makers—typically, people with titles of manager, director, vice-president, president, or CEO—are charged with making all kinds of decisions that contribute to the fundamental economic missions of their firms. They evaluate continually and make decisions based on their evaluations. Rarely do they evaluate and act in a manner comparable with the theories and practices of program evaluators, who have a public sector orientation. Evaluation experts usually focus on examining effects of programs (Phillips, 1983; Parker, 1986). Corporate decision makers focus on making up-front choices (Swanson and Gradous, 1988). One simple way of viewing these differences is to think of the decision maker as a venture capitalist who makes big business decisions on selected information. In contrast, the professional evaluator is viewed as an accountant who tediously adds up the pennies already spent. The bold venture capitalist relies on quick timing and choosing the best option, while the cautious accountant waits for all the data before filing an accurate report.

The discrepancy between the needs of the decision makers in business and the solutions espoused by many evaluation theorists is so great that I regularly ask the provoking question, "Will program evaluation scholars like this?" If the answer is no, I then consider that I might be on the right track.

The Nature of the Private Sector

A number of conceptual models describe the business context in which private sector training operates. The Tichy, Frombrun, and Devanna (1982) model is comfortable for both business people and scholars. The elements of the firm, according to this model, include mission and strategy, organizational structure, and human resources management. The societal forces include political, economic, and cultural factors.

For an analogy, we can use the conceptual model of the firm as the subject matter and the evaluator as a photographer. The photographer chooses among cameras; some have lenses that can zoom in or out. This lens movement, plus other intricacies of a camera and its operation, metaphorically represent the evaluator's expertise and toolbox. To the typical evaluation expert, the end produced—the picture—is the evaluation report. To the industrialist, the evaluation report is only *one* means to some other end within the business milieu of the firm. Many other things are going on in the firm, typically more than can be reasonably comprehended. Thus, the private sector decision maker agonizes about the options, their potential contribution to the business mission and strategy, and the relative cost and benefits of each option.

In my personal life I most often choose the simplest solution that will yield me the quality standard I desire. To return to the camera metaphor, my personal camera is a $79.95 model. The relative costs (financial and operational) and benefits (picture quality) of my daughter's $300 camera do not even interest me. I could take up two pages explaining why the $79.95 camera is perfect for me. However, most photography experts tend to snub my $79.95 solution. When they criticize, I simply cut those camera experts out of my photography decision-making process. Similarly, program evaluation experts are regularly cut out of the private sector training activity. Occasionally, at the training department's equivalent of the photographer's "weddings and proms," the experts are invited in to provide evaluation services. For example, the new human resources director, who manages all the human resources functions and who has no expertise in training, may hire an outside consultant to evaluate the training department. Another example would be the training manager who hires an external evaluator to assess the effectiveness of a company-wide, participative management training effort.

It is important to note, so as to round out the scenario, that evaluation experts are also critical of the typical training-evaluation practices in the private sector and what they generally see as training-evaluation practices that contain major threats to validity (Campbell, 1971; Parker, 1986).

Efficiency and Effectiveness

The general business decision framework embraces the values of effectiveness and efficiency. Most public sector decision makers use the rhetoric of effectiveness and are constrained by controlled costs. Managers in the public sector are generally more verbal than their private sector counterparts. The public sector managers "talk" their way into success, and private sector managers "perform" their way into success. Thus, the public sector rhetoric often gets way out of line with the available resources. Since public sector rhetoric and accountability are with different constituencies, the loop is rarely closed as it is in the private sector.

In an elementary way, efficiency can be thought of as the cost side of the formula, and effectiveness the benefit side. In the private sector, however, return-on-investment (ROI) reigns supreme. Within firms, some business units are directly connected to benefits (or income generation), and others are considered overhead costs (or burden). For the training department positioned as overhead, cost control is paramount. A good training manager in this context reduces the training budget. When training is positioned as a business partner, that is, as a person expected to directly increase profits, performance improvement related to the goods and services provided by the firm is critical. A good training manager in this context increases units of work performance that have value to the firm. A very obvious example is with a firm that sells training as a product and service. A U.S. producer of portable data collectors used for statistical process control of manufactured goods also sells data collector training and statistical process control training to its hardware customers. The training manager reports to the national sales director and is evaluated on his or her dollar sales of training. Additionally, the training manager has financial incentives in the form of a commission beyond the base salary.

Most firms are not in the business of training employees or customers except when doing so contributes directly to the total performance of the organization. It is costly to train people. If possible, training, as with any other high-cost activity that is not making an important performance contribution, will be eliminated from the corporate budget. Decision makers generally decide to support training as a business decision with the purpose of improving performance, maintaining performance, or fulfilling compliance requirements.

In some instances training is forced on an organization by law or by regulatory agencies. For example, many chemical, manufacturing, and service industries are required by law to train employees in handling chemicals in order to protect their workers and the general public. Likewise, a small custodial firm can be held legally accountable for informing its employees about and protecting them from the cleaning agents they use in their work. The controversy surrounding the asbestos industry has been well publicized and has gained great public attention. Lives have been lost as a result of exposure to asbestos and asbestos-producing firms have been economically crippled or put out of business as a result of litigation.

Compliance training is a serious matter, and the role of evaluation is to document that the training did, in fact, take place. Even so, documentation such as content outlines, samples of handout materials, and attendance records will likely exceed the evaluation required for compliance training. Such crude evaluations as attendance at safety training, when viewed through the photographer metaphor, are analogous to a child's use of a cheap plastic camera containing film that develops before her eyes—instant documentation. The photographs may be fuzzy and poorly framed, but they are good enough for the situation.

Foundations of Training

A number of years ago I presented the notion that there are two foundational bodies of knowledge for training: psychology and economics (Swanson, 1982, 1987). In a more recent discussion of the role of training and organizational performance, Campbell (1988) acknowledges this perspective. The psychological (educational) foundation of training is primarily focused on the development and implementation of training. The economic (managerial) foundation focuses on the organizational needs assessment and the ultimate contribution of training to organizational performance.

When performed correctly, systematic training in industry and business does not start with the assumption that there is a need for training. Many scholars of education, as well as those who articulate the dominant public sector view, assume that education or training is needed. In contrast, private sector training begins by questioning the need for improved organization or individual performance, then further questions the probability that reality training will influence that performance. Training systems, such as the Training Technology System (see Figure 1), carefully connect the training function to performance at both ends of the system (Swanson, 1987).

The learning, human development perspective is the view held by the majority of the practitioners in the training profession. Concurrently, the economic performance, or human capital view, is the perspective held by the majority of the private sector decision makers, who most likely were not trained to be trainers.

Private sector training-evaluation efforts are framed by the two foundational areas of economics and psychology and by the quest for effi-

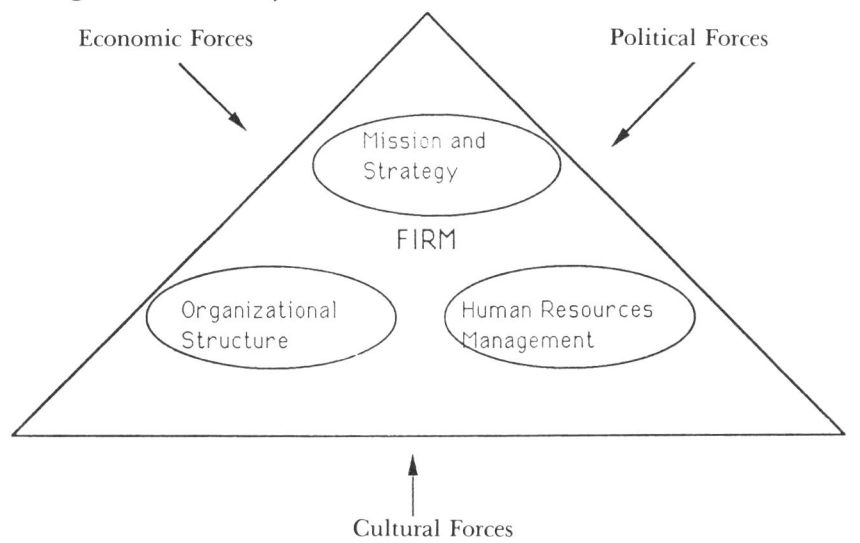

Figure 1. The Tichy, Frombrun, and Devanna Model for the Firm

Source: Tichy, Frombrun, and Devanna, 1982. Reprinted by permission of *Sloan Management Review.*

ciency and effectiveness. These four elements provide a useful matrix for examining training evaluation (see Table 1).

Most program evaluation experts focus on the psychological row of the matrix in terms of behaviors or processes of changing behaviors. This psychological focus, by itself, can be fundamentally out of line with the private sector economic agenda.

The psychology-efficiency cell focuses on speeding up the learning process or on utilizing fewer resources in a set time period through the application of sound learning theory and educational technology. Another way of increasing efficiency is to reduce the inefficiencies of and barriers to learning that typically exist in unstructured training, such as self-managed, trial-and-error-learning.

Evaluation at the efficiency level is process-oriented and formative in nature. Such evaluations are used to improve the training/learning process. The substance of process control and improvement evaluation activity is important for professional trainers but is of little interest to nontrainers and others whose perspective primarily represents the economic/business concerns of organizations.

The economic-efficiency cell focuses on reducing or containing costs. Almost all businesses have fairly elaborate cost-accounting systems and methods. Furthermore, most work groups are financially monitored by someone in their respective firms. Categories of costs include fixed, variable, direct, charge-back/overhead and marginal/step costs (Head, 1985; Swanson and Gradous, 1988). Training departments and other departments seen as overhead are closely monitored through management information systems for the purpose of controlling costs or spotting cost-cutting opportunities. Even while this monitoring is going on, it is not common for this cost information to be fully shared with the training department or the personnel being evaluated. Furthermore, it is very possible for management to establish a training cost-reduction or cost-containment goal without directly communicating this to the training manager. At the present time there are many corporate takeovers in process in American business. Many of these firms, in an attempt to retain

Table 1. Training-Evaluation Framework

Productivity	Foundations of Training	
	Economics	*Psychology*
Efficiency	Reduce or maintain dollar/performance cost	Reduce or maintain trainee anxiety
Effectiveness	Maintain or increase dollar/performance benefit	Maintain or increase trainee expertise

their existing ownership status, will systematically cut staff and functions for the purpose of lowering costs and increasing profits. Units not directly connected to the economic-efficiency cell are candidates for such cuts. Human resource departments in these firms that are grounded in the "psychology only" perspective are invariably cut.

The competent training manager, working in a cost-reduction or cost-containment environment, can increase training quantity and quality by entertaining new alternatives. Evaluation should help plan and verify these efforts. Creative managers can look at high-cost items such as especially costly programs or costly phases of programs and begin brainstorming options, evaluating these options to see if they deliver comparable results. Since training-development and delivery costs can be very high, the use of an "off-the-shelf" program may save on development costs. Self-instruction also may save on delivery costs. The development of new partnerships with the stakeholders in the training context, thus sharing responsibility for training, may also reduce costs. The point is, given the many training options available, there are possibilities for providing the same performance results at reduced costs. This kind of thinking is private sector thinking and the kind that evaluators should help trainers to pursue.

For example, the service training department of a manufacturing organization faced such a cost-containment condition. The department had been providing "free training" to independent distributors. In response to their cost-containment goal, they produced programmed instruction and trained their distributors to manage the training. They realized an $80,000 cost reduction, which they reinvested in other opportunities.

Learning and Satisfaction

The psychology-effectiveness cell in Table 1 is familiar to most evaluation experts (Brinkerhoff, 1987), the associated techniques being well developed and widely used. Here the focus is on trainee satisfaction and learning. The traditional, private sector training-evaluation practice of measuring participant satisfaction and the public sector practice of measuring participant learning are well understood by both professional trainers and evaluation experts. Trainers are often seen by evaluation experts as giving too much credence to measures of trainee satisfaction, while trainers generally believe that evaluation experts overemphasize formal measures of learning (Sleezer, 1989). As an additional difference, I have also observed that most private sector trainers live in a culture of "customer satisfaction," whereas most public sector educational evaluators live in a culture of "gains in knowledge."

Trainers generally focus learning measures on the very specific work behaviors that they are expected to develop in employees. They thus provide in-training exercises to satisfy trainees and others that learning has taken place. Some examples of specific work behaviors are the following: (1) Managers need to know the purpose of the XYZ Corporation employee-appraisal system and the method of completing the forms. (2) Aluminum extruder operators need to know how to start up, operate, troubleshoot, and shut down the "ACME Extruder."

To ensure effective work behaviors in these and other specific domains, trainers emphasize up-front analysis of work behavior to make sure the content is right (Swanson and Gradous, 1986; Carlisle, 1986). They then construct tests to check whether this content has been learned. In-training performance and performance tests (to a lesser extent) are valued over after-the-fact tests of knowledge.

Attempts to simplify the measures of satisfaction and to expand the measures of satisfaction beyond the trainees to the trainee's supervisors are frequent among private sector trainers (Swanson and Sleezer, 1987). For example, lengthy satisfaction questionnaires, often seen in public sector education programs, are reduced to the core purpose of training and core values of the organization. Core questions for participants typically include the following: Was the training delivered professionally? Were the learning objectives met? Was the original need met? Was the training valuable? Core questions for the participant's supervisor would *only* include the last two items. This is because supervisors did not directly experience the training.

Clearly, there are multiple "customers" of training in the business context and they should be taken seriously by trainers. Supervisors that allow their employees to go to training pay a price. That price is sometimes a direct budget transfer and almost always includes time away from regular work (which still needs to be completed). To ignore this decision maker in the training process would be very shortsighted.

Economic Effects

The economic-effectiveness cell in Table 1 is the bugaboo of the training profession and has not been well developed by evaluators. The evaluation options in this cell range from the accountant's perspective (Flamholtz, 1985) to the venture capitalist's perspective (Swanson and Gradous, 1988). Each financial perspective provides a powerful view of the position of training in the organization. To a top manager, not being able to talk about training from a financial perspective is almost worse than having inaccurate numbers. The private sector culture is a financial numbers culture. If trainers cannot even attempt to talk about their corporate activities in terms of financial indices, they are almost automatically placed off to the side or "out of the ballpark." If they can talk financial numbers, right or wrong, they are at least "in the ballpark." Once there, they and others can refine the measures.

Top managers in business and industry view and value training through an economic lens. These nontraining decision makers will mentally fill in the financial picture on training with or without the actual financial data. The risk is that, in most instances, this off-the-cuff analysis is inaccurate and not supportive of training.

As the cost and demand for training have increased, the demand for financial data on training is coming from top management, not from training professionals. But there are some promising new trends. One important method that some training professionals are using to move into the "economic-effectiveness" cell is the use of a training-for-performance orientation. Through critical investments in up-front training needs analyses, trainers identify important performance opportunities and needs that training can solve (Rossett, 1987). Subsequent back-on-the-job increases in performance provide excellent proxies for economic effectiveness in business and industry. Once the training opportunities and needs are isolated and pursued, the evaluator obtains actual measures of performance in the workplace. So it was with a very large health maintenance organization. After struggling with how to measure the effectiveness of a company-wide organizational development effort to "be nice to the customer," they finally came down to the numbers of subscribers as the performance measure. That is, the "nice/not nice" impression eventually translated to customer subscriptions. In this instance, the human resources development program and the measure of effectiveness were at the heart of the organization.

The key to the economic-effectiveness perspective is to get trainers to focus on "performance needs" and to get corporate decision makers to "want" what they need. A "wants" analysis will surely yield very specific requests for training programs, and going around asking people what they want is easy and comfortable. But very often those wants have nothing to do with the performance needs or problems that organizations and individual employees face because careful performance analysis is not required by the "wants" assessment. For example, managers in a large manufacturing firm said that they wanted cross-training for all their production employees to help cover work during absences and vacations. At the very same time, an incredible 48 percent of their product was turning out as scrap. For any number of reasons, the employees did not even know their own jobs, let alone their neighbor's jobs. The need for operator training was great. The need for operator cross-training was minimal given the urgent quality control problem.

Most important aspects of businesses already have been evaluated. Examples include units produced, cost per unit, accident-free days, sales per salesperson or sales region, number of customers, scrap rates, customer satisfaction, dollar sales, and a variety of other quality indices. Since most important aspects of firms are evaluated, the training evaluator may only need to look at ongoing organizational or employee-performance measures before and after training to get at the appropriate economic effectiveness measures. Of course, evaluators still must work before and after training to link training results to these important aspects of business.

Summary

An understanding of the language of the private sector is critical to evaluators. The evaluation expert who plans to work in the private sector should refer back to the opening sentence of this chapter: "The mission and goal of business and industry are to maximize the economic return on investment through the production and sale of goods and services." Clearly, the values and vocabulary of business differ greatly from the values and vocabulary of traditional public sector evaluation.

One simple, but important, means to understanding the full and realistic potential of training evaluation is to study the values and the vocabulary of business and industry. I believe that such an effort will change the evaluation expert's view of evaluation and increase the expert's potential for improving training in industry and business. Two concrete personal examples include the business and industry concepts of auditing and process improvement.

I worked in Brian Murphy, a business person, on the concept of auditing training (Murphy and Swanson, 1988). This was a very direct effort at taking the business language and methods of financial auditing and using them to develop a process for auditing the training function in the private sector. We sampled each step of the training process to see whether there were departures from sound practices. Only where such departures were identified was further evaluation (a costly process) pursued. New priorities, not just new words, appeared. Furthermore, the information generated from this auditing process did not exceed the requirements of the decisions to be made.

A second example is when I worked with Catherine Sleezer in the area of training-process improvement and control (Sleezer and Swanson, 1989). We were working with an electronics manufacturing firm that has a complex manufacturing system in need of a great deal of process control to keep it running (and to improve it). Conceptually, we identified a similar need for a training-process control system for the training department, and important new evaluation ideas emerged for us. In both of these examples, the values and language of the businesses involved greatly influenced the training-evaluation language and methods we proposed.

A second simple, but important, means of understanding the full and realistic potential of training evaluation is to study the existing measures of performance in any one business or industry. The title of this chapter contains the clue: "Everything important in business and industry is evaluated." While this statement is most likely an exaggeration, I have witnessed too many evaluation experts running around trying to invent measures that are compatible with their own values. Evaluation experts should cull the performance measures already used in and valued by firms. Training that is not connected to these measures should be questioned, and evaluation of training should incorporate these measures.

Evaluation of the effectiveness of an ongoing training program in terms of existing measures of organizational and individual performance is a powerful means of getting a firm to think critically about the purpose of training (Swanson and Sleezer, 1987). In the process, decision makers often ask, "Why did we approve this program?" At that point, the training and nontraining personnel are usually ready to think about training as a means to some large business goal, and evaluation as a way of helping to make wise decisions along the way.

References

Brinkerhoff, R. O. *Achieving Results from Training: How to Evaluate Human Resource Development to Strengthen Programs and Increase Impact.* San Francisco: Jossey-Bass, 1987.

Campbell, J. "Personnel, Training, and Development." *Annual Review of Psychology,* 1971, *22,* 565-595.

Campbell, J. "Training Design for Performance Improvement." In J. P. Campbell and R. J. Campbell (eds.), *Productivity in Organizations: New Perspectives from Industrial and Organizational Psychology.* San Francisco: Jossey-Bass, 1988.

Carlisle, K. *Analyzing Jobs and Tasks.* Englewood Cliffs, N.J.: Educational Technology, 1986.

Flamholtz, E. G. *Human Resource Accounting: Advances in Concepts, Methods, and Applications.* San Francisco: Jossey-Bass, 1985.

Head, G. *Training Cost Analysis.* Boulder, Colo.: Marlin Press, 1985.

Murphy, B. P., and Swanson, R. A. "Auditing Training and Development." *Journal of European Industrial Training,* 1988, *12* (2), 13-16.

Parker, B. L. "Summative Evaluation in Training and Development." *Journal of Industrial Teacher Education,* 1986, *23* (2), 29-55.

Phillips, J. J. *Handbook of Training Evaluation and Measurement Methods.* Houston: Gulf Publications, 1983.

Rossett, A. *Training Needs Assessment.* Englewood Cliffs, N.J.: Educational Technology, 1987.

Sleezer, C. M. (ed.). *Improving Human Resource Development Through Measurement.* Alexandria, Va.: American Society for Training and Development Press, 1989.

Sleezer, C. M., and Swanson, R. A. "Is Your Training Department Out of Control?" *Performance and Instruction,* 1989, *28* (5), 22-26.

Swanson, R. A. "Industrial Training." In W. H. Mitzel (ed.), *Encyclopedia of Educational Research.* (5th ed.) New York: Macmillan, 1982.

Swanson, R. A. "Training Technology System: A Method for Identifying and Solving Training Problems in Industry and Business." *Journal of Industrial Teacher Education,* 1987, *24* (4), 7-17.

Swanson, R. A., and Gradous, D. B. *Performance at Work: A Systematic Program for Analyzing Work Behavior.* New York: Wiley, 1986.

Swanson, R. A., and Gradous, D. B. *Forecasting Financial Benefits of Human Resource Development.* San Francisco: Jossey-Bass, 1988.

Swanson, R. A., and Sleezer, C. M. "Training Effectiveness Evaluation." *Journal of European Industrial Training,* 1987, *11* (4), 7-16.

Tichy, N. M., Frombrun, C. J., and Devanna, M. A. "Strategic Human Resource Management." *Sloan Management Review,* 1982, *23,* 47-61.

Richard A. Swanson is a professor and director of the Training and Development Research Center at the University of Minnesota, St. Paul.

Linking business issues and decision making to training evaluation activities determines the overall success of training efforts.

Evaluation and Business Issues: Tools for Management Decision Making

Dale C. Brandenburg

The purpose of this chapter is to outline some general application issues of evaluation of training in business settings. Included are a general definition of evaluation, a review of recent literature, including a synopsis of the current status of training evaluation, and a look at what is being performed in business and industry in the name of evaluation.

We begin with a definition of evaluation as the collection of data used as information for decision making. What is central in this simple definition is that the goal of evaluation is the linking of information to business issues. To illustrate this definition, I refer to some typical questions posed by writers in the business evaluation literature. Brethower and Rummler (1979) present a systems view of the organization to illustrate that training must not be viewed in isolation from its functional environment, that is, the organization. Also, in their view, evaluation is an information-gathering and decision-making process. Questions are posed on what might be measured, the dimensions of measurement, the sources of data, alternative data-gathering methodologies, and evaluation criteria. The benefits from applying such a systems approach include applicability across a wide variety of training situations as well as ability to "tailor" the evaluation plan to the situation. Thus, only the important questions are selected in order to obtain the required information for any one evaluation application.

Alden (1978) begins his model with the following question: Will management even consider making a decision about whether or not to change a program or how it will be changed? In focusing on the evaluation process, Alden asks what research questions will provide the needed data, what level of data is practical and important to management, and, finally, what criteria will management use to make their decisions. Thus, the need for management commitment before evaluation start-up is critical to prevent the collection of data for which there is no meaningful use. Morrison (1981), in his management orientation model, poses the following two questions: What decisions does each individual make, and who needs the information on training programs? Morrison characterizes a set of decision-making levels where low-level decision making requires more specific information, and higher levels require more global information.

As a final illustration, Putnam (1980) lists a set of eight questions in which the first two are the following: What are the results of the evaluation intended to be used for, and what kinds of information count with decision making? The remaining questions focus on practical issues of data collection, analysis, and constraints. It is worthwhile to note that these authors take a pragmatic approach to evaluation which assumes that management is not overwhelmingly concerned with exactitudes and that management is aware of the degree of uncertainty in evaluation data. From this short review, it can be discerned that a primary focus for training evaluation is the linking of business issues in the form of questions to the formulation of some explicit management decisions.

This linkage of the evaluation process to business issues is exemplified in Hunter and Nassauer's (1982) description of the evaluation unit at Arthur Andersen and Company. This company's view of evaluation is the making of rational decisions based on evidence, and the most important issue to guide the approach is the answer to the following question: What is the business problem? This question and their view of evaluation imply that evaluation is supportive of the training effort and that training is supportive of the business goals. Evaluation in its many forms provides the link from the actual training or other intervention back to the work setting and lets the business manager know whether or not the business problem has been solved. From a line manager's perspective, the issue with regard to evaluation is simply, did my problem go away?

A couple of examples serve to illustrate the importance of business issues. In an organization that prepares professional staff for a variety of functions in the field, an instructional designer and an evaluator decide on information needs for the pilot of a new course. One critical factor required from the pilot (before the course reaches the area field offices throughout the country) is that it must have a good reception among the professionals attending. The business issue under consideration, then, is to assure that the pilot course has the same quality and standards expected with existing courses. It would be a business risk to "roll-out" a course if the quality, as viewed by a representative sample of the target audience, was much lower than others currently available.

As a second example, a training manager in manufacturing wishes to gather information about the return-on-investment for a series of courses in statistical process control. Information available for analysis includes results of experiments run by the engineers who have been trained in the use of the techniques. Prior to the implementation of these courses, little in the way of formal knowledge regarding statistical process control was utilized by the employees. Thus, the training manager can be fairly certain that uses of the techniques can be attributed to this particular training. Because the training materials for the statistical process control course were quite expensive, the training manager wants to know how much value is obtained by the plant site through the use of these materials. In similar settings throughout a number of plant sites, parallel data collection is being performed. The results of this evaluation will be forwarded to corporate headquarters for collation and summarization. The business issue underlying this effort was whether or not these materials would be worthwhile for dissemination throughout the entire corporation; that is, what is the expected value added to the organization from the use of these materials?

New Terms for Familiar Functions

One of the differences a student of the business training evaluation literature and the educational evaluation literature will note is that the business literature tends to be more *future-anchored*, whereas the education literature tends to be *past-anchored*. Alternatively, one can say that business training evaluation is conducted in order to move forward on a set of defined issues, whereas educational evaluation is usually a post hoc analysis to decide what was good or bad about a past intervention. Since the late 1960s when Scriven (1967) differentiated formative and summative evaluations, educational evaluation has provided the generally accepted heuristic. In contrast, business training procedures, while similar to educational procedures, tend to use slightly different terms. It is common to view business functions as input, process, and product (or output) because these terms correspond to the general language of the business culture.

Generally, evaluation methodology associated with products is different from that associated with input and process. The terms gaining greater acceptance in business training are *quality control* for input and process functions and *quality assurance* for the product or output functions. Quality control is used in the sense that a business uses it to control the internal processes prior to a product being rolled out or ready for field implementation. Quality assurance reflects evaluation done on the product itself. Acceptance in meeting standards of customers and clients and provision of value-added impact for the organization are examples of quality assurance. The terms quality control and quality assurance can be used in a somewhat similar manner to that of formative versus summative evaluations. One major concerted effort over the past few years, as we shall see later in the chapter, is in the development of new techniques and methods for the quality control area. This development has been primarily directed at input types of mechanisms, which are associated with analysis of the educational or business situation in which a training intervention needs to take place.

Review of the Current Status of Evaluation

The purpose of this section is to provide a brief review of the current status of training evaluation. Information for this review was taken from a talk I gave at the National Society of Performance and Instruction Conference (Brandenburg, 1988) a study by Smith (1984), a study by LDG Associates (1986), and preliminary versions of the American Society for Training and Development and Department of Labor (forthcoming) research projects (hereafter ASTD/DOL).

Within each of these studies, there is an attempt to discern expert opinions about why evaluation is more important at present than it was in the recent past. Generally, four reasons are given: growing cost pressures in training units, changes in technology, need for qualified people, and intense competition from abroad.

The experts also indicate more emphasis for using the terms quality assurance and quality control for the evaluation process. These labels are viewed as more than just lip service. When the evaluation process is referred to as part of quality assurance or quality control, it is likely to involve line management, it is a concerted attempt to decrease the historical distrust of the training unit, and it reflects the increased effort to improve instructional products before training is rolled out. This distrust has many sources, including the educational backgrounds of training practitioners being different from the backgrounds of others in the organization. The case in many organizations is that the training unit became a "dumping ground" for those individuals who could not contribute otherwise to the organization, and the use of techniques and terminology within training was not well understood nor appreciated by organizational decision makers. To initiate training-evaluation activities in such settings would require adept lobbying efforts by training managers.

Thus, quality assurance or control can be viewed, on one hand, as a reaction to a relatively checkered history in the application of evaluation methods to training.

From the ASTD/DOL studies we note that major pressures to evaluate training are really internal to the organization. This internal application of evaluation methods can be inferred by examining who performs the majority of evaluations. Both the Smith and LDG studies point out that the course developer is the number one person doing the evaluation, and the training manager is second. The involvement of line managers in training evaluation is most often a secondary consideration if at all. This internal use of evaluation is also reinforced with the kinds of techniques that are utilized. In general, the two major techniques are (1) in-class questionnaire, and (2) in-class skill test or knowledge test. Techniques that would be used to follow up on a training intervention, such as posttraining feedback, on-the-job observation, or supervisor opinions obtain low-usage rankings. From the ASTD/DOL studies, one notes that 100 percent of evaluation projects reportedly use reaction measures, whereas 30 percent use some other techniques (for example, written tests, self ratings) to measure learning, and 15 percent were devoted to either behavior or results data collection activities. Thus, the apparent business decision for which evaluation data are collected both from the LDG and ASTD/DOL studies points toward either program development or program modification as the target. On the one hand, it is not surprising to note that evaluation data would be collected in conditions most under the control of training practitioners, that is, the internal classroom or other controlled environment. Alternatively, it can be argued that these forms of data collection do little to verify needs analysis data or to record on-the-job applications.

To get more specific on particular evaluation techniques, it is useful to examine the table created by Smith (1984) and published in a monograph by Brandenburg and Smith (1986). It is reproduced here as Table 1. Smith catalogued 331 evaluation studies reported in the *Training and Development Journal* and *Performance and Instruction* over a fifteen-year period. These results show that the student was the main focus of evaluation, more specifically, student acceptance and student learning. Those two columns in Table 1 represent almost 57 percent of the total number of measures. The major conclusion from these data is that external measures, for example, job behavior and organizational results, are used far less than the internal criteria of student reactions and learning.

One trend that has been noted in studies by Smith and LDG, is an improvement in terms of the number of techniques used in a given evaluation study. Over the past twenty-five years the median number of techniques has increased from around 1.7 per study to 2.3. Thus, the typical study uses at least two or three measures. Another trend noted from

Table 1. Summary of Data Collection Techniques by Criteria

Summary Of Data Collection Techniques By Criterion / Techniques	Content Relevance	Design Quality	Delivery Quality	Student Acceptance	Learning	Retention	Attitude Change	Post-PGM Behavior	Value	Cost or Efficiency	TOTAL
Professional Judgment	2	21						1		1	25
Needs Or Task Analysis	5						2				7
Participant Opinion, Self-Report	3		4	110	9		3	27		1	157
Paper-And-Pencil Test					144	18		2	2		166
Performance Test, Job Simulation, Role Play					16			7			23
Frame Errors Or Progress Tests					28						28
Physiological Measures					1						1
Course Or Project Records (Time, Cost, Grades)					5	8		1		39	53
Instructor Rating Or Opinion		2			4	4				1	11
Classroom Observation			5		1						6
Attitude Instrument					3		23				26
Boss Opinion	1							28	1		30
Subordinate Opinion								6			6
Peer Opinion								4			4
Job Observation	1							2			3
Product Evaluation								4	1	1	5
Organizational Results, Measurements								4	31	1	36
Customer Opinion								2	2		4
TOTAL	12	23	9	123	210	18	27	89	37	43	585

Source: Brandenburg and Smith, 1986.

the LDG study has been more involvement from line or operating managers in evaluation. This includes using line managers as advisory panels to be surveyed immediately after training, informal meetings, and at three-to-six-month follow-up interviews. In the Smith data of Table 1, less than 10 percent of the selected measures were "boss opinion."

Another encouraging result comes from the LDG and ASTD/DOL studies of what it takes to ensure a successful evaluation. These studies agree that evaluation strategies need to be integrated early on in the development process and that successful evaluations are planned and structured early at the needs analysis stage. In addition, the evaluation strategies and techniques are designed early in the development process. Data must be relevant and presented in a simple form for management, which argues for a good systematic set of reporting guidelines. Thus, understanding client concerns and then designing the evaluation to meet them is the preferred current approach, which promises that evaluation will pay close attention to business issues.

As an example, in one large company that I worked with, the results of a needs analysis pointed toward the development of a course in marketing skills for a certain classification of individuals. Because of the delay in time from the completion of this analysis to the first version of the instructional materials, a checklist was created to obtain line management reaction to the topics of the training course. The checklist was a list of errors commonly made by personnel under the direction of these managers, and the managers were asked to judge whether or not the elimination of these errors would improve overall work group performance. As such, this use was a verification of the needs analysis, but it also provided the managers with a means to evaluate improvement in job performance once their personnel returned from training.

One confounding issue noted by practitioners has been that the state-of-the-art evaluation methodology is adequate, but it still is not always implemented in day-to-day practice. Such methodology is impractical, it is argued, because of the following constraints: time, money, lack of management support, lack of evaluation expertise, and unnecessarily rigorous research designs. Field demands for quickness, shortcuts, and practicality in evaluation methods continue to be a significant concern.

The LDG and ASTD/DOL studies, as well as a dissertation by Gutek (1988), point out some implications for future developments in training evaluations. The most needed areas appear to be coordination with line management and field-based follow-up of information. There is a need for better tools for needs assessment, and a need to tie evaluation to objectives in business planning. Senior practitioners would like to see more practical, less rigorous evaluation methods and quicker techniques to get at the transfer of training. Gutek notes that while training directors know what good evaluation ought to be, they do not achieve it because of one of the following two reasons: they do not make it a priority, or they have not educated their managers on how the evidence can be obtained.

Another trend in the training-evaluation literature can be noted from the number of recent books wholly devoted to the topic. Among these are May, Moore, and Zammit (1987), Brinkerhoff (1987), Swanson and Gradous (1988), and the forthcoming publication of the ASTD/DOL research project. All four of these efforts represent significant extension and understanding of the evaluation process as it is practiced in business and industry. The book by May and colleagues, three Digital Equipment Corporation employees, contains fifteen chapters of original writings on topics ranging from strategic planning to case studies of curriculum evaluation. Discussion is devoted to some fairly sophisticated techniques and applications of evaluation that have recently been pursued in business and industry. The Brinkerhoff book is a description of his six-stage model, with a number of very practical applications and illustrations of how the model can actually tie evaluations to business decisions as well as produce quality instructional products. Significant emphasis is placed on how to structure a comprehensive evaluation, with descriptions of numerous techniques to employ. Swanson and Gradous present a new technique that should be considerably important for training managers as they face accountability issues. The authors' approach is to put the emphasis for examining the benefits of training up front at the needs analysis stage so that optimal choices for training alternatives can be undertaken and the net return estimated before the project actually begins. The ASTD/DOL research represents the first comprehensive attempt at summarizing the status of both the measurement and accountability aspects of evaluation.

In summarizing this section on the status of training evaluation, we can note a discrepancy between theory and practice. One way to examine this discrepancy is to note who is saying what. On the one hand, we have training practitioners saying that "quick and dirty" techniques are needed in order to get the job of evaluation over with in the least painful manner. The developers of the evaluation models referred to at the beginning of this chapter and the book authors reviewed immediately above are training managers, former training managers, and academics. The latter tend to argue for more attention to the front-end processes of evaluation, where line managers can express initial buy-in for training. As I have pointed out elsewhere (Brandenburg, 1989), if professionals in human resource development do not understand the line manager's function and expected outputs, the technology of evaluation will either languish unused or not be applied to appropriate objects. Advanced evaluation concepts can help practitioners demonstrate to line managers how training helps solve managerial problems. New training tools should be viewed, therefore, as assistance in the attainment of business goals.

Evaluation Application Matrix

As I indicated earlier, the many applications of evaluation in business and industry training can be subdivided into the two major categories of quality control (focus on training process) and quality assurance (focus on results). These two general levels of application can be further divided by looking at the objects of evaluation. In general, there are five: the employee, the intervention or course, the program or curriculum, the human resources development (HRD) organization, and the total organization. This matrix of the two levels of activities across the five objects is depicted in Table 2.

Each cell of the matrix contains labels for techniques or methods used to collect data for evaluation decisions. Note that under quality control for a course we find the primary techniques indicated earlier in

Table 2. Evaluation Application Matrix

Object	*Quality Control*	*Quality Assurance*
Employee	Diagnosis Remediation Skill building	Certification Proficiency Master job performance
Intervention or Course	Course development Instructor evaluation Vendor evaluation End-of-course performance Cost forecasting Media production evaluation	Course impact Transfer of training Validation field testing Cost effectiveness
Program or Curriculum	Program development Program improvement Monitoring of ongoing courses	Field effectiveness Cost-benefit analysis Implementation evaluation Impact evaluation
HRD Organization	Client satisfaction Training unit credibility Performance audit of unit	System impact studies Program audit Performance appraisal Productivity measurement
Total Organization	Front-end analysis Management audit Skills-mission consistency	Culture change Organizational performance audit Contribution to bottom line

the brief review. These two top left-hand cells produce information for course development, media evaluation, instructor evaluation, and student learning. If we examine the previous review of the literature with regard to this matrix, we can note that the majority of evaluation takes place in the top three cells of the quality control area. It was evident from that review that much lip service was given to the quality assurance aspects of the intervention or course level and the program or curriculum level. The latter reflect course impact, transfer of training, and effectiveness in the field.

On the other hand, if we consider where the most needed techniques for future emphasis lie in working with line management and in tying evaluation to business needs, applications are required for quality control in the bottom two cells. Very few significant field-based efforts have been reported for performance audits, front-end analysis of organizations, or management audits. Conceptual approaches to these topics have been appearing recently in the literature and thus indicate a trend to link more directly the organizational goals to training.

One example of a technique to provide a front-end analysis for organizational change efforts is the cross-impact evaluation technique given by Hunter (1988) and employed by Arthur Andersen's change-management unit. The purpose of cross-impact analysis is to identify important information within an organization's culture and environment that will assist a project team in identifying priorities and bottlenecks for change efforts. The strategy is to compare the present status of the organization to what will exist after the change is in place. Variable domains for investigation include organizational design, culture, job design, infrastructure, and person/machine interfaces. The introduction of new technology or new organizational structure can be examined by noting what impact it may have in an ideal environment when matched with its associated transformed state. Furthermore, the "crossing" of present to future states is captured through interactions within the organization. This highly detailed front-end analysis technique should prove useful for examining complex organizational interventions, such as computer-assisted design (CAD) systems in manufacturing. The results of a cross-impact analysis conducted on the implementation of CAD may point out that the jobs of other individuals change more than the job of design engineer, which the CAD system was intended to change. This in turn suggests job design modifications for a considerable number of individuals within the manufacturing plant.

While training managers and training practitioners appear quite concerned with the issues of transfer of training, recent literature has focused more on quality control and other kinds of front-end techniques. For example, cost-benefit analysis as a quality assurance technique is used at the course or program level, but recent attention given to cost-benefit forecasting as a quality control technique (and thus a front-end process) reflects this change in emphasis. This is not to say that quality assurance techniques are less important, but detailed studies using them remain quite costly to perform. For a case in point, Arthur Andersen's professional education division has a large and diverse evaluation staff, yet less than 20 percent of their courses undergo some form of impact evaluation. Most effort is expended in typical course evaluation, with significant attention to needs analysis and verification. Quality assurance techniques also suffer from the problem of cause attribution. That is, a determination of whether or not training or any other HRD intervention can be the sole cause for personal or organizational change is problematic and unproductive because training results make only a partial contribution to overall performance.

The absence of a cause-and-effect relationship in field-based, uncontrolled (in a statistical sense) training environment has both a positive and a negative side. Negatively, it becomes difficult and politically disruptive to attribute results to programs or people, and thus training managers cannot take credit for their department's efforts. One the other hand, a systematic attempt at implementing quality assurance studies will reap long-term benefits to the organization in terms of learning what works and what does not. Such studies that use impact evaluation techniques, cost-benefit analysis, and other field effectiveness processes can accumulate evidence over time to pinpoint variable domains of most importance when formulating strategy for a given type of intervention. For example, by systematically collecting customer satisfaction ratings in a commercial construction company, the amount of rework was cut by 30 percent by introducing a standard form to communicate customer-requested changes in projects. When implemented over a long period of time, the use of this change form resulted in the revision of a training course for first-line supervisors.

The capacity to perform quality assurance studies becomes especially important when technological changes (machines or otherwise) are introduced into an organization. The more expensive or global the changes, the more likely quality assurance studies are required in order to learn how operating units within an organization adapt to new technology. The introduction of quality programs (for example, statistical process control) is an example of efforts in which it is generally known that education and training begin with top executives and progress through various cycles to the production workers.

One important way to use the matrix in Table 2 is to transform its cells into business-related issues to which evaluation can provide an answer. Once the issue is defined and its location within the matrix is identified, the methods of data collection can be readily limited to an appropriate few. To illustrate, consider a typical question posed by a client: Are course participants achieving the objectives? The answer entails a quality control measure of the trainee, typically quantified by an observation (or performance) checklist or multiple choice test. Here are a few other examples:

1. *Issue:* Is the course as designed intended to meet identified needs?
   Cell: Quality control of the course
   Typical methods: Line manager review of materials, analysis/design review by selected target participants
2. *Issue:* Has the course eliminated the training need, or has the business problem been solved?
   Cell: Quality assurance of the course
   Typical methods: Follow-up interview with line managers, records or documentation of trainee performance
3. *Issue:* Has the HRD organization provided an acceptable rate of return over the past two years?
   Cell: Quality assurance for the HRD organization
   Typical methods: Program audit matching course, curriculum, and unit objectives to accomplishments measured by management and organizational documentation.

By phrasing questions that guide the evaluation process and by tying the process to the application matrix, two benefits are possible. First, an acceptable method or technique for collecting the data can be identified, and, second, the primary audience for the resulting information should become known. These two results assist in planning the evaluation and providing information about how a report of results may be structured.

A second type of use for the evaluation matrix is as a scoping mechanism for identifying business risks associated with a given evaluation plan. Evaluation studies that cover more than three cells of the matrix are very unlikely. In fact, many good ones target only one or two particular areas and are still comprehensive in answering questions needed for those areas. Thus, a targeted evaluation plan that uses the matrix will assist in getting at the important business decisions and will avoid the risk of too many questions to answer sufficiently. By transforming the need for information into evaluation issue questions and then referring to the matrix, it is possible to identify interrelationships that may be missed by conducting a less focused investigation.

On the basis of the above discussion, one may conclude that the difference between training evaluation and educational evaluation is similar to the difference between degree of focus and comprehensiveness. Partly owing to time and resource constraints, training evaluation studies are likely to be shorter and less comprehensive than educational evaluation studies. For example, in a training program designed to teach new employees how to put together circuit boards, the outcome to be measured was how quickly these employees could assemble two good circuit boards every three days. How these employees reacted to the training or how well they interacted with their supervisors were of little concern in this particular case. The business issue, getting new employees "up to speed" as quickly as possible, was the primary evaluation focus.

Current Challenges

Thus far I have attempted to describe the field of training evaluation as it is currently practiced by discussing the discrepancies between theory and practice, the emerging role for line management in making training evaluation increasingly more responsive to business needs, and the emphasis on development of new techniques for front-end analysis (quality control). I would now like to turn attention to three challenges facing evaluation in business and industry in the 1990s. These challenges are change management, new technologies in the workplace, and general functional integration of analysis and design activities.

First, let us examine change management. The fact that Arthur Andersen's consulting division has been renamed "change management" signifies, I believe, an important trend in American industries that wish to be competitive in the global marketplace. If there is anything constant for the 1990s, it is likely to be change. New organizational structures, decentralized decision making, transformed organizations, more diversity in the background of workers, and shortages of both unskilled labor and highly skilled labor are current buzzwords and projected demographics. These conditions offer challenges to organizational structures and demand attention to the management of change as an important discipline. Currently, we evaluators have devoted less effort to this area than have our organizational development counterparts. We need to merge techniques and better understand each other in order for this function to flourish in the future. Evaluation offers numerous opportunities for the creation of new techniques and processes that will have a direct impact on how an organization does its work, as well as on a number of worthwhile research endeavors that are likely to lead to innovative practices both inside and outside the training area.

As I view this set of conditions, there exist two possible directions for merging training-evaluation expertise with organizational development expertise. One direction is methodological and the other is content specific. Because the content-specific options are associated with given industry segments or topic domains, detailed discussion of them is beyond the scope of this chapter. Examples of such domain-specific activities are quality circles, organizational realignments for hospitals, and new work systems for steel mills. In the methodological area, one example is Hunter's (1988) cross-impact analysis strategy, and another is organizational mapping (Rummler, 1986). Organizational mapping uses the open systems approach to "map" an organization according to how it gets its work done, as opposed to the standard hierarchical organizational chart. Using this technique, the four basic inputs to any organization—capital, technology, raw materials, and human resources—are examined in terms of their flow through the organization as a system. Two benefits of employing the technique include provision of a conceptual model for approaching the task of reorganization and provision of a model of an organization wherein alternative systems flow and reporting relationships can be systematically examined and evaluated.

A third example of a methodology was formulated by the staff of the Industrial Technology Institute and is depicted in Figure 1. This diagram is used to explain the relationship of business issues to the "upskilling" of the work force for potential clients. In typical fashion, our clients often jump from problem to solution without considering the drivers of their organization (its strategies, goals) or how training—or, in this case, the upskilling of production employees—needs to be linked to existing components of their respective organizations. One of the issues we see, as shown in Figure 1, is that training is a considerable distance, psychologically and sometimes physically, from business strategy. For example, in a training needs analysis study, it became apparent that if the employees were upskilled to use new equipment and tools, then the organization could suffer serious labor-management problems. One reason for this projection was that after the employees were trained, the types of work for which the employees were now suited did not exist within their current markets. Management was ill prepared to seek these new markets. Second, these new skills required the purchase of new tools that the organization was not prepared to buy. These are just a couple of examples of how the linking of training to business issues could save the organization considerable grief *before* attempting their change effort.

The second challenge to future evaluation considers new technologies in the workplace that will have a profound impact. Some have viewed this concern as "the rich will be getting richer and the poor will be getting poorer." Those who understand little about the computer and its impact on work will be left far behind those that have already progressed a couple of generations beyond the simple desktop PC. The fact that new kinds of technology will be entering both manufacturing and service industries means that dramatically more training will have to be taking place on new systems. These new systems are different than many of the older technologies already in the workplace. They are different because their impact of implementation is not nearly as isolated as experienced with earlier machines and tools, that is, secondary effects could be considerably greater than the primary area for which the technology was designed. A simple example may help to clarify. The introduction of computer-assisted design (CAD) in manufacturing was thought to greatly

Figure 1. Strategy and Context for Training Needs Assessment and Evaluation in Large Manufacturing Plants

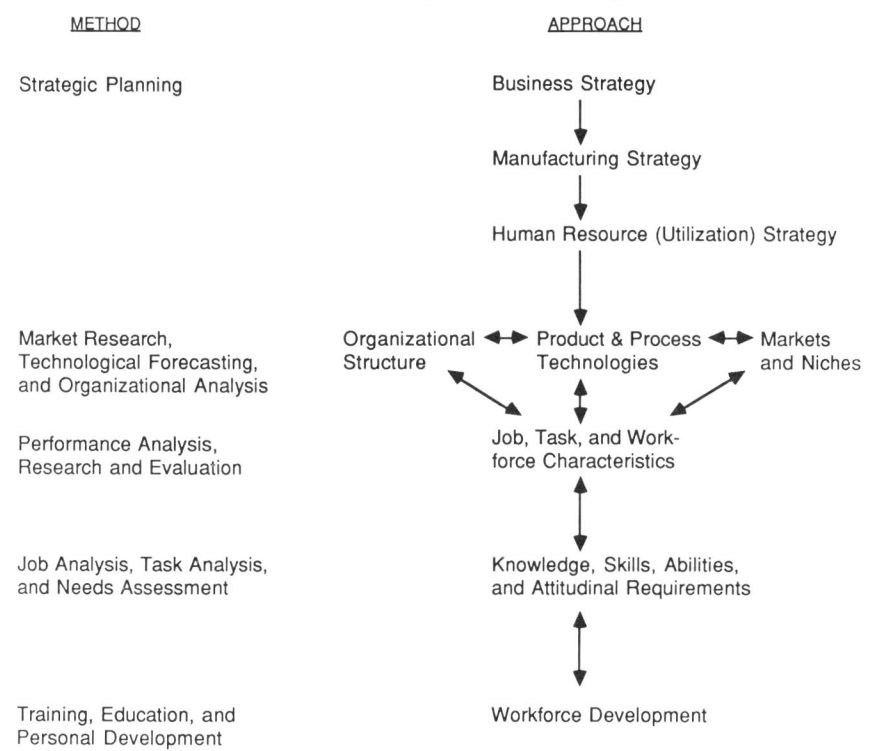

METHOD	APPROACH
Strategic Planning	Business Strategy ↓ Manufacturing Strategy ↓ Human Resource (Utilization) Strategy ↓
Market Research, Technological Forecasting, and Organizational Analysis	Organizational Structure ↔ Product & Process Technologies ↔ Markets and Niches
Performance Analysis, Research and Evaluation	Job, Task, and Workforce Characteristics
Job Analysis, Task Analysis, and Needs Assessment	Knowledge, Skills, Abilities, and Attitudinal Requirements
Training, Education, and Personal Development	Workforce Development

Source: Industrial Technology Institute, Training and Development in Manufacturing Program, 1989.

aid both the efficiency and quality of designs produced by industrial design engineers. What was not planned for with the use of CAD workstations was the impact on other engineers, which has been shown to be significantly greater than on the targeted design engineers. A recent study by McAlinden (1989) demonstrated that the impact of CAD systems on all engineers was virtually triple what it was for design engineers in terms of dollar sales increase. What happened in the typical case where CAD systems were introduced was that production and manufacturing engineers (those who actually implement the designs on the shop floor) were much more easily able to make changes in the design to reflect constraints of production machinery or other characteristics. Prior to the introduction of CAD, such "tweaking" of designs and the cycling back to design engineers were much more costly in terms of overall throughput time and labor.

Another area where new technologies are affecting business is close to home, the training function. The promise of new techniques such as computer-based training, interactive video disks, and hypertext has led to a mushrooming market for products that attempt to fulfill the promise of the hardware. What has happened for the most part has been a tremendous increase in relatively poor courseware (or other types of software) and other gadgets in the guise of peripherals, all with abundant promises. Professional evaluators can have an important role in distinguishing fad from substance.

The third area of challenge to evaluation contains some elements of the previous two. What I believe I am detecting is an emphasis for evaluators to upgrade their skills in the analysis and design components of human performance interventions. If training evaluators are then more prized in the marketplace, the more likely their skills and talents will be used in front-end kinds of techniques.

The new technologies, physical as well as informational, will require more thorough investigation of how they can be integrated into systems without disrupting performance of individual components (human and otherwise). The issue of suboptimization will be an important consideration for evaluators. Suboptimization occurs when a portion of a larger system is changed to reflect the needs of only its components, without considering the overall impact on dependent subsystems. In a plant producing silicon wafers, for example, a problem in polishing the wafers was encountered. By eliminating the polishing problem, a backlog was subsequently caused in the cutting area so that the overall output from the facility remained the same. Careful up-front evaluation could have predicted and then helped to eliminate this problem by recommending more training in the cutting area to handle more wafers.

Thus, the redirection of evaluation from looking only at the end components to looking more toward developing future integrative relationships is likely to be prized in the business setting. We, as evaluators, need to understand more about the variety of analysis techniques to assist us in working with our instructional design colleagues. Concurrently, we need to form appropriate alliances with the organizational development experts in structuring organizational redesign, work redesign, and job redesign so that new instructional or other interventions will have a compatible environment. And, third, in working with line management, we need to take into account true business needs and true business risks in identifying our proposed solutions.

References

Alden, J. "Evaluation in Focus." *Training and Development Journal*, 1978, *32*, 46–50.
American Society for Training and Development. *Best Practices: What Works in Training and Development* (excerpts), forthcoming.

Brandenburg, D. C. "The Status of Training Evaluation: An Update." Paper presented at the National Society for Performance and Instruction Conference, Washington, D.C., April 9, 1988.

Brandenburg, D. C. "Issues for Professional Practice." In R. Swanson and C. Sleezer (eds.), *The Contribution of Measurement Science to Training.* Washington, D.C.: American Society for Training and Development, 1989.

Brandenburg, D. C., and Smith, M. E. *Evaluation of Corporate Training Programs.* Report no. 91. Princeton, N.J.: ERIC Clearinghouse on Tests, Measurements, and Evaluation, 1986.

Brethower, K. S., and Rummler, G. A. "Evaluating Training." *Training and Development Journal,* 1979, *33,* 14-22.

Brinkerhoff, R. O. *Achieving Results from Training: How to Evaluate Human Resource Development to Strengthen Programs and Increase Impact.* San Francisco: Jossey-Bass, 1987.

Gutek, S. "Training Program Evaluation: An Investigation of Perceptions and Practices in Nonmanufacturing Business Organizations." Unpublished doctoral dissertation, Western Michigan University, 1988.

Hunter, R. H. "Technology Change and Assimilation." Paper presented at the National Society for Performance and Instruction Conference, Washington, D.C., 1988.

Hunter, R. H., and Nassauer, R. I. "Implementing Training Course Development Evaluation in a Corporate Setting: A Case Study." Paper presented at the National Society for Performance and Instruction Conference, Detroit, Michigan, 1982.

LDG Associates, Inc. *What Companies Do to Evaluate the Effectiveness of Training Programs.* Gardner, Mass.: LDP Associates, 1986.

McAlinden, S. P. *Programmable Automation, Labor Productivity, and the Competitiveness of Midwestern Manufacturing.* Ann Arbor, Mich.: Industrial Technology Institute, 1989. (Prepared for the Economic Development Administration of the U.S. Department of Commerce.)

May, L. S., Moore, C. A., and Zammit, S. J. *Evaluating Business and Industry Training.* Boston: Kluwer-Nijhoff, 1987.

Morrison, G. R. "Developing Evaluation Programs for Industry." Paper presented at the Annual Meeting for the American Educational Research Association, Los Angeles, California, April 1981.

Putnam, A. O. "Pragmatic Evaluation." *Training and Development Journal,* 1980, *34,* 36-40.

Rummler, G. A. "Organization Redesign." In M. E. Smith (ed.), *Introduction to Performance Technology.* Washington, D.C.: National Society for Performance and Instruction, 1986.

Scriven, M. *The Methodology of Evaluation.* American Educational Research Association Monograph Series on Curriculum Evaluation, no. 1. Skokie, Ill.: Rand McNally, 1967.

Smith, M. E. "Trends in Training Evaluation." Paper presented at the National Society for Performance and Instruction Conference, Atlanta, Georgia, April 1984.

Swanson, R. A., and Gradous, D. B. *Forecasting Financial Benefits of Human Resource Development.* San Francisco: Jossey-Bass, 1988.

Dale Brandenburg is senior researcher at the Industrial Technology Institute, a private research and development organization promoting the modernization of manufacturing firms. In addition to publishing in the area of training evaluation, he is chair of the National Society for Performance and Instruction Emerging Technology Committee and consulting editor for Performance Improvement Quarterly.

Index

A

Albrecht, K., 6, 19
Alden, J., 84, 98
Alkin, M. C., 37, 42
American Society for Training and Development (ASTD), 64, 98
American Society for Training and Development and Department of Labor (ASTD/DOL) research projects, 86-91
American workers, skill deficiency of, 36
Arnoff, S., 60, 69
Arthur Andersen and Company, 7, 84, 92-95; Evaluation Services Unit (ESU) at, 47-57; Management Information Consulting Division (MICD) at, 47; Professional Education Division (PED) at, 45-57
ASTD/DOL. *See* American Society for Training and Development and Department of Labor
AT&T, 1

B

Bassock, M., 32, 33
Bernhard, H. B., 36, 42
Blank, W. E., 60, 70
Brandenburg, D. C., 9, 11, 19, 60, 70, 86-91, 99
Brethower, D. M., 24, 28, 29, 33
Brethower, K. S., 83, 99
Brinkerhoff, R. O., 24, 28, 29, 33, 77, 81, 90, 99
Business issues: and application matrix, 91-95; data collection techniques and, 87-89; evaluation of, 83-98; upskilling workers, 96-97

C

Campbell, J., 73, 74-75, 81
Capps, C. J., 64, 70
Carlisle, K., 78, 81

Carnevale, A. P., 1, 4, 5, 36, 42
Change management, described, 95
Computer-assisted design (CAD), 6; in manufacturing, 96-97
Computer-based training, 98
Content-specific activities, 95
Control Data Corporation, 71
Corporate-centered training programs, 7-8
Cost-benefit analysis, 92-95
Course development evaluation, 48-52; elements of, 50-51; outline of typical report in, 51; three summary points in, 51-52
Cross-impact analysis, purpose of, 92

D

Daillak, R., 37, 42
Data collection techniques, summary of, by criteria, 87-89
Deming, E. W., 17, 19, 67, 70
Desatnick, R. L., 6, 19
Devanna, M. A., 72, 75, 82
Dickinson, A. M., 32, 33
Domain-specific activities, 95

E

Effectiveness, as key training issue, 47-48
Eurich, N. P., 1, 4, 5, 19
Evaluation: application matrix, 91-95; building training commitment through, 35-42; and business issues, 83-98; current challenges in, 95-98; data collection techniques, 87-89; defined, 60, 83-84; internal, 45-57; review of current status of, 86-91; of sales training, 21-33; of training by trainers, 59-69; transforming training through, 5-19; understanding, 71-82; user-focused, 36-40. *See also* Training evaluation
Evaluation application matrix, 91-95

101

Evaluation criteria, for sales training, 24-27
Evaluation cycle, 29
Evaluation literature, 45, 54-55, 83-98
Evaluation questions, 27-28; causal, 29-31; comparative, 30-31; and evaluation cycle, 29; faultfinding, 30; merit of sales training, 28; political problems in, 31-32; and sales-training cycle, 28-29; and worth of sales training, 27-28
Evaluative statements: about sales training, 22-24; beliefs influencing, 23-24; consequences of, 23; primitive, 22-23
Experimental-design-based evaluation, 12-13
External evaluators, 45, 59-60

F

Feeney, E. J., 32, 33
Flamholtz, E. G., 78, 81
Follow-up evaluation, 48
Ford Motor Company, 10
Fortune 500 corporations, 8, 13-14
Frombrun, C. J., 72, 75, 82
Front-end analysis, for organizational change, 90-95
Future-anchored, business literature as, 85-86

G

Gainer, L. J., 36, 42
Gilbert, T. F., 10, 19
Glaser, R., 32, 33
Global marketplace, 6-7, 95
Gradous, D. B., 72, 76, 78, 81, 90, 99
Greer, M., 28, 33
Grider, D. T., 64, 70
Gropper, G. L., 70
Gutek, S. P., 1, 4, 9, 19, 89, 99

H

Hahne, C. E., 28, 33
Hayes, G. E., 6, 19
Head, G., 76, 81
Hluchyj, T., 24, 29, 33
Hunter, R. H., 84, 92, 95-96, 99
Hypertext, 98

I

IBM, 1, 7, 49
In-class tests, 87
Industrial Technology Institute, 96-97
Ingols, C. A., 36, 42
Interactive video disks, 98
Internal evaluation strategies, 45-57; course development and, 49-52; and evaluation literature, 54-55; evolution of, 53; factors contributing to effective, 52-53; organizational context of, 46-47; overview of, 47-49; suggestions for effective, 55-57; techniques of, 87

J

Jerrell, J. M., 59, 70
"Just-in-time inventory," 6

K

Kirkpatrick, D. L., 9, 19, 36, 42, 60-61, 63, 67, 70
Knowles, M. S., 63, 70

L

Labor shortages, future, 6-7, 95
LDG Associates, Inc., 86-91, 99

M

McAlinden, S. P., 97, 99
Madaus, G. R., 33
Management: business decision framework of, 73-74; commitment to training by, 35-42; and decision making, 83-98; and evaluation theorists, 71-72; and financial numbers, 78-80; human capital view of, 75-77; and sales training, 32-33; and training evaluation, 16; and upskilling workers, 96-97
Management auditing, 26-27
May, L. S., 68, 70, 90, 99
Meltzer, A. S., 36, 42
Minnesota Ballet, 71-72
Mirman, R., 28, 33
Moore, C. A., 90, 99

Morrison, G. R., 84, 99
Murphy, B. P., 80, 81

N

Nassauer, R. I., 84, 99
National Society of Performance and Instruction Conference, 86-91
Needs assessment, 48, 89, 90; in manufacturing plants, 96-97
Needs-driven training, 8-9, 15
Northwest Airlines, 71
Nowakowski, J. R., 24, 29, 33

O

O'Brien, R. M., 32, 33
Odiorne, G. S., 32, 33
Organizational mapping, 95-96
Operations auditing, 26-27

P

Parker, B. L., 72, 73, 81
Past-anchored, business literature as, 85-86
Patton, M. Q., 37, 42
Pearlstein, G., 65, 70
Performance analysis, in training evaluation, 66-67
Performance and Instruction, 87
Peters, T. J., 6, 20
Phillips, J. J., 72, 81
Pillsbury Company, 71
Private sector training, 72-74, 80-81
Productivity, defined, 64-65
Program-driven training, 8-9, 15
Putnam, A. O., 84, 99

Q

Quality assurance, 85-98
Quality control, 85-98
Quality management, in training evaluation, 67-68

R

Resnick, L. B., 32, 33
Return-on-investment (ROI), 35-36, 73-74
Robinson, D. G., 8-9, 20

Robinson, J. C., 8-9, 20
Ross, P. A., 70
Rossett, A., 79, 81
Rummler, G. A., 29, 32, 33, 66, 70, 83, 95-96, 99
Ruyle, K. E., 26, 33

S

Safety training, 74
Saint, M., 28, 33
Sales training: asking the wrong questions about, 29-32; business issue and, 32-33; evaluating, 21-33; evaluation criteria in, 24-27; evaluative statements about, 22-24
Sales-training cycle, 28-29
Scriven, M. S., 27, 33, 85, 99
Skills, knowledge, and superficial attitudes and beliefs (SKA), 10
Sleezer, C. M., 28, 33, 77-78, 80-81, 82
Smith, M. E., 9, 20, 60, 70, 86-91, 88, 99
Staelin, J. R., 32, 33
Stakeholders, 23-24, 31
Steelcase, 7
Stufflebeam, D. L., 33
Swanson, R. A., 9, 14, 20, 28, 33, 72, 74-78, 80, 81-82, 90, 99

T

Tests and measurement, 48
Tichy, N. M., 6, 20, 72, 75, 82
Toombs, L. A., 64, 70
Trainee feedback, 9-10, 62-63, 66, 87
Trainees, learning and satisfaction of, 77-78
Trainers: as evaluators, 59-69; factors affecting evaluation practices of, 62-66; and financial numbers, 78-80; formative evaluation practices and, 65-66; methodological problems of, 61-62; and trainee testing, 63-64; and training products, 64-65; and work behaviors, 77-78
Training: bureaucratization of, 7-8; challenge to, 5-6, 19; current context of, 6-11; curricula in, 8-9, 15; customer service and, 15-16; economic effects of, 78-80; efficiency

Training *(continued)*
and effectiveness of, 73-74; foundations of, 74-77; model for, 75; private sector, 72-74; problematic characteristics of, 10-11; professionalization of, 8; public vs. private sector, 71-72, 77-78; sales, 21-33; three zones of, 13-14; trainee satisfaction spiral in, 9-10

Training and Development Journal, 87

Training and Development in Manufacturing Program, 96-97

Training evaluation: by trainers, 59-69; current challenges in, 95-98; developmental environment in, 17-18; effectiveness issues in, 55; focusing on targets in, 16-17; four-stage model of, 36-37; framework, 75-76; future of, 11; growth and development of, 56-57; literature, 83-98; and management, 16; of management quality control points, 55-56; in manufacturing plants, 96-97; misplaced efforts in, 11-14; new terms for, 85-86; performance analysis in, 66-67; practices, 60-66; private sector, 78-81; promising directions in, 14-15; proof fallacy in, 11-13; quality control and management approach to, 17; quality management in, 67-68; review of current, 86-91; success factors in, 56; trainee reactions to, 62-63; and training alternatives, 18-19; user-focused, 36-42; zones, 13-14

Training literature, 59-62, 69; formative evaluation in, 60; summative evaluation in, 60-61
Training targets, 16-17
Training Technology System, 75
Training-inherent problems, 10-11
Transfer of training, 91-95
Tryouts of training, 65-66

U

University of Minnesota, 71-72
Upjohn, 7
User-focused evaluation, 36-40; application of, 40-42; creating recommendations for, 39-40; data collection and analysis in, 38-39; design of, 38; implementing recommendations in, 40; reporting, 39; stages of, 37-40

V

Validity, as key training issue, 47-48

W

White, P., 37, 42

X

Xerox, 7

Z

Zammit, S. J., 90, 99
Zemke, B., 6, 19